I0425133

Alexander McGillivray

and the Creek

Confederacy

The Struggle for the Southern

Backcountry

R. Michael Pryor

Copyright 2010, 2012, 2015 by R. Michael Pryor

All rights reserved.

No part of this publication may be reproduced or transmitted
in any form or by any means, electronic or mechanical,
including photocopying, recording, or any other information
storage and retrieval system, without permission of the
author.

ISBN-10   1-4537-6107-1

ISBN-13   978-1-453-76107-6

Pryolino Press

Chicago, Illinois 60614

Printed in the United States of America

To that which I treasure the most, Tiffany

For all of her love, laughter and support

Also by R. Michael Pryor

Teaching for Recall & Analysis:
New Strategies for Improving Student Achievement in Social
Studies

Teaching for Recall & Analysis:
Advanced Floor Timelines for U.S. History

Teaching for Recall & Analysis:
Advanced Interactive Venn Diagrams for U.S. History

Teaching for Recall & Analysis:
Improving Student Achievement in World History

Essential American Principles:
A User's Guide to American Documents

CONTENTS

Timeline – History of the Southeastern Region

1521 - 1559 Spain makes three unsuccessful attempts to establish colonies to the north of New Spain in the southeastern region of North America. Southwest Florida in 1521, Georgia in 1559, and Gulf coast near Pensacola in 1559.

1540 - 1599? Spanish military conquest and European diseases destroy most of the indigenous population in the southeastern region.

1565 St. Augustine is established by the Spanish and becomes the first permanent settlement in North America. The city is the oldest continuously occupied European-established settlement.

1562 - 1563 French explorers landed near the St. Johns River (Florida) on May 1, 1562. They establish the colony of Charlesfort in present-day South Carolina. The colony eventually fails and is abandoned.

1584 - 1587 Sir Walter Raleigh secured a charter from the Queen of England to settle lands in North America. The colony (Roanoke) in present-day North Carolina eventually fails and is abandoned.

1600s The Creek Confederacy is formed from the remnants of surviving southeastern tribes.

1619 First African slaves arrive in Jamestown, Virginia. By 1700, African slaves become the primary source of bonded labor in British North America.

1666 - 1681 French explorer LaSalle claims the entire Mississippi River drainage basin for France. New France's territorial claims extended from the Hudson Bay to Louisiana.

1700	Britain has established numerous colonies on the eastern coast of North America.
1715 - 1717	Yamasee War: a conflict between the British settlers in the Carolinas and the various Native American tribes of the southeastern region. Major battles occurred in present-day Georgia and South Carolina. By the end of the war, the Yamasee tribe is greatly weakened which allows for the establishment of Georgia.
1716	France establishes Fort Rosalie along the Southern portion of the Mississippi River (present-day Natchez, Mississippi).
1720s	The members of the McGillivray Clan immigrate to colonial South Carolina.
1729	The Carolinas are divided into North and South Carolina.
1733	The colony of Georgia is founded by the British. James Oglethorpe arrives in January 1733 at mouth of the Savannah River and establishes the town of Savannah.
1750	Likely birth year of Alexander McGillivray. He is born near present-day Montgomery, Alabama.
1754 - 1763	French and Indian War: France losses the war is forced to surrender most of its North American territorial holdings to Britain and Spain.
1775 - 1783	American Revolution: American colonists gain their independence from Britain. During the war Alexander McGillivray is commissioned as an officer in the British Army.

1783	Treaty of Paris: The treaty formally ends the American Revolution and the United States of America is established. The British government stops providing the Creek Confederacy with military protection.
1783	Lachlan McGillivray, Alexander's father, returns to Scotland. He is forced to flee due to his pro-loyalist sympathies.
1784	Treaty of Pensacola between Spain and the Creek Confederacy. Spain promises to protect Creek territorial rights in Florida and guaranteed access to European trade goods.
1783 - 1786	Treaty of Augusta (1783), Treaty of Galphinton (1785), & Treaty of Shoulderbone (1786). The state of Georgia gains land that formally belonged to the Creek Confederacy. The Creeks will challenge the legitimacy of these treaties.
1790	Treaty of New York in which the United States promises to defend Creek territorial rights. Firmly establishes McGillivray as the leader of the Creek Confederacy.
1793	Alexander McGillivray dies from an illness in Pensacola, Florida on February 13, 1793.

Map -- 18th Century Southern Backcountry

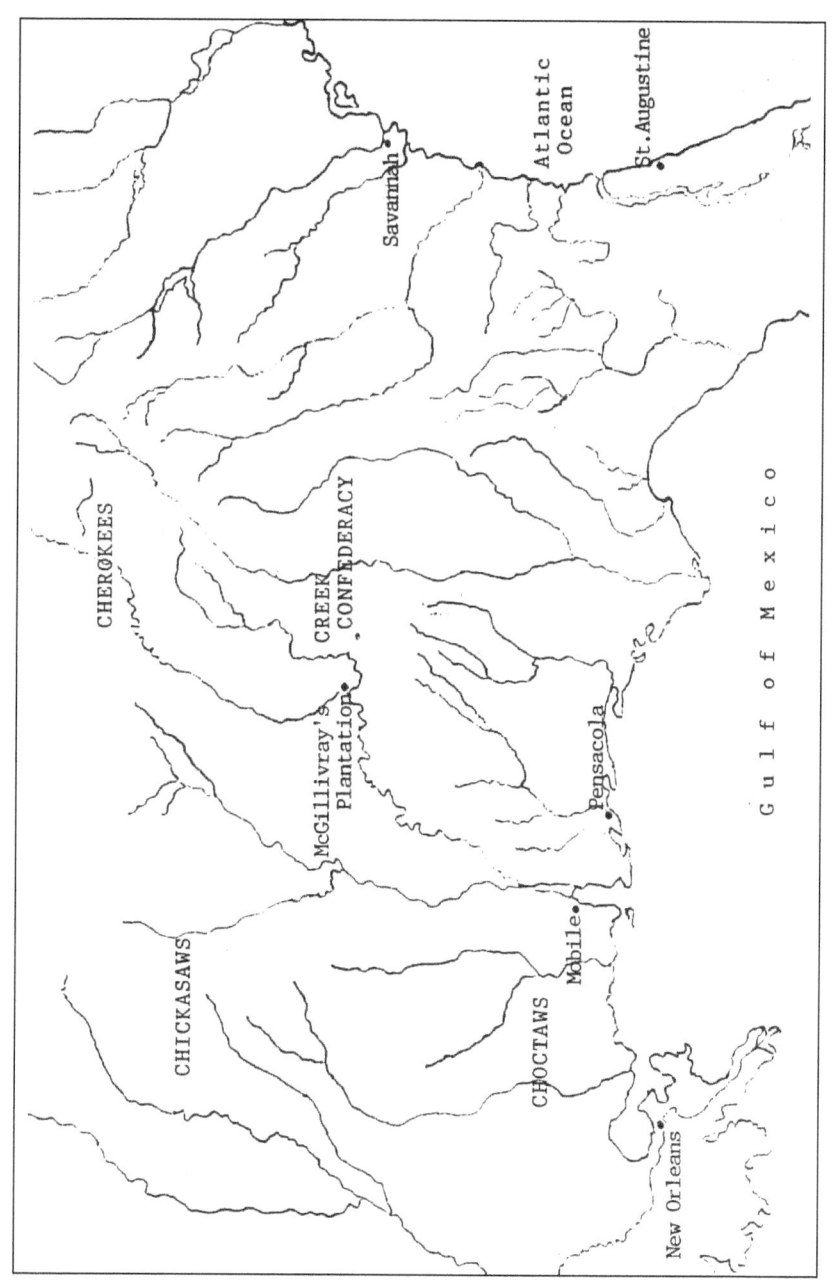

McGillivray's Paternal Family Tree

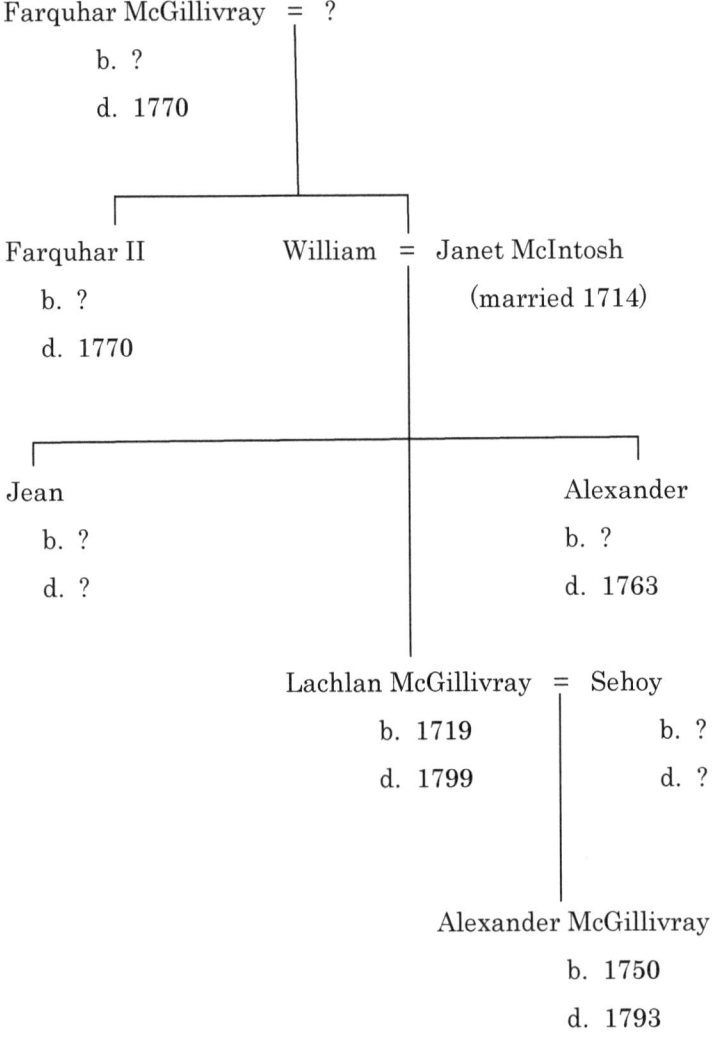

Farquhar McGillivray = ?
      b. ?
      d. 1770

Farquhar II   William = Janet McIntosh
  b. ?   (married 1714)
  d. 1770

Jean   Alexander
  b. ?   b. ?
  d. ?   d. 1763

Lachlan McGillivray = Sehoy
      b. 1719   b. ?
      d. 1799   d. ?

Alexander McGillivray
      b. 1750
      d. 1793

Alexander McGillivray

and the Creek

Confederacy

The Struggle for the Southern

Backcountry

"We certainly as a free Nation have a right to choose our protector…"

- Alexander McGillivray, 1784

Prologue

♦

The Process of Cultural Coalescence

Alexander McGillivray, a Native American leader, became a central figure in the Southern backcountry during the territorial struggles of the late-eighteenth century. In order to defend the borders of the Creek Confederacy he used an amazing mixture of political shrewdness, economic monopolization, and diplomatic finesse. The son of a successful Scottish merchant and a member of an influential Creek Indian clan, his success arose from an ability to learn from, and utilize, a variety of political, ethnic, and economic relationships.

During McGillivray's relatively brief life of forty-three years he was commissioned as a British officer, a Spanish colonel, and an American brigadier general. However, throughout all of these seemingly conflicting positions he maintained an unyielding pro-Native American identity. His kinship relationships and acquired diplomatic skills created a broad web of political and economic connections. Each "strand" of this web connected to a multiplicity of sources, from Creek and Scot to Spanish and American. In many ways, McGillivray was a politically well-positioned American mestizo who skillfully applied the resources which were available to him. This complex merging of political, economic, and ethnic relationships by Alexander McGillivray is essentially defined as a process of *cultural coalescence*.

However, the concept that ethnic and cultural relationships were an advantage in diplomatic negations is a relatively new topic. Traditionally, eighteenth-century Southern history explored the coastal regions, focusing upon the experiences of European colonists and the institution of African slavery. Historical research about the interior of the Southeast before the Revolutionary War is limited, and often reflects a perspective which treats existing Native American populations as curious oddities. One of the first historical works that challenged this stereotype was David H. Corkran's The Creek Frontier, 1540-1783, published in 1967. Corkran's work, however, still primarily focuses upon the influence of Europeans on the Southeastern region.[1]

The social and ethnohistory approaches of historians like Gary B. Nash, James Axtell, and William Cronon have allowed scholars to reevaluate backcountry/frontier relations during the colonial period. Colonial North America is no longer remembered as a place of polarized extremes, with stereotypes of civilized colonists conquering savage Native American tribes. Instead a myriad of cultural groups existed, with terms like "civilized" and "savage" possessing little meaning. In reality, political alliances were created and maintained out of both friendship and necessity. Some historians have applied this new understanding to help recreate a deeper understanding of the Southern backcountry. Works by James H. Merrell and Daniel H. Usner Jr. display this cultural complexity of the eighteenth-century Southeast.[2]

Alexander McGillivray was born into this politically and socially complex region. Although numerous contemporaries and

[1] David H. Corkran, The Creek Frontier, 1540-1783, (Norman: University of Oklahoma Press, 1967).

[2] James H. Merrell, The Indians' New World: Catawbas and Their Neighbors From European Contact Through the Era of Removal (New York & London: W.W. Norton & Company, 1989); Daniel H. Usner Jr., Indians, Settlers, & Slaves in a Frontier Exchange Economy (Chapel Hill: University of North Carolina Press, 1990).

historians have noted McGillivray's important role in Southeastern political alliances, few full length biographies exist about the Creek Indian leader. The most well-known researcher on this topic is John Walton Caughey's 1959 book and Michael D. Green's 1980 essay.[3]

Few historians have linked McGillivray's political and diplomatic skills directly with his cultural background. However, one can argue that McGillivray's success arose impart due to his diverse social/cultural background that can only be described as *American mestizo*, which were people of European and Native American ancestry who have been largely been ignored by U. S. scholars. As the son of a Scottish immigrant and Creek Indian, McGillivray inherited a rich set of traditions and kinship networks on which he skillfully built his leadership position.[4]

Chapter one analyzes McGillivray's formative years by exploring his parents and their various kinship networks. The next two chapters explore the early rise of the Creek Indian's political career as a British officer, Creek leader, and later as an economic broker in the Southeastern region. Chapter four examines McGillivray's influences and his rapid expansion of political power due to his connections to Scottish business interests and the Spanish government. The final chapter investigates the McGillivray's political and economic apex with the leader

---

[3] John Walton Caughey, McGillivray of the Creeks, (Norman: University of Oklahoma Press, 1959); Michael D. Green's "Alexander McGillivray" in R. David Edmunds, Studies in Diversity: American Indian Leaders, (Lincoln and London: University of Nebraska Press, 1980); Edward J. Cashin, Lachlan McGillivray, Indian Trader: The Shaping of the Southern Colonial Frontier (Athens: University of Georgia Press, 1992) provides a good historical account of Alexander's father and the McGillivray clan.

[4] Thomas D. Watson, "Strivings For Sovereignty: Alexander McGillivray, Creek Warfare, and Diplomacy, 1783-1790," Florida Historical Quarterly 58 (April, 1980): 400-414; J. Leitch Wright Jr., "Creek-American Treaty of 1790: Alexander McGillivray and the Diplomacy of the Old Southwest," Georgia Historical Quarterly 21 (December, 1967): 379-400; Arthur Preston Whitaker, "Alexander McGillivray, 1783-1789," North Carolina Historical Review 5 (April, 1928): 181-203.

negotiating a treaty between the Creek Confederacy and the United States in 1790. Ultimately, McGillivray's life displays an evolution of political and economic power; all of which led to what can only be describing as a *coalescence* of cultural influences.

McGillivray, by the end of his short life, had temporally halted the expansion of Georgia's western border and arranged a powerful treaty with the recently formed United States of America, while simultaneously maintaining a similar treaty with Spain. The leaders of the United States, Georgia, Spain, as well as other neighboring Native American societies, as a whole; only occasionally cooperated with each other. Yet all of these parties, by 1790, actively pursued a friendship with McGillivray, who possessed the ability to juggle and maintain these seemingly incompatible alliances. McGillivray's uncanny ability to create and sustain these contradictory relationships is an enduring testament to his skill as a shrewd and determined Native American leader.

Chapter 1

♦

The Formative Years: 1750 - 1775

In the 1700s, the Southern backcountry was a multi-linguistic and ethnically diverse region. Colonist, and increasingly African slaves, inhabited the Atlantic coast and the piedmont region; while various Native American societies dominated the Appalachian highlands and interior woodlands. During the colonial period, the southern backcountry included an area that stretched from the mountainous piedmont of the Carolinas to the marshes of Northern Florida. This loosely defined region extended west from vast the pine forest of Georgia to the banks of the Mississippi River.

During the seventeenth century colonist, mainly of English ancestry, had migrated to the coastal plains of the Atlantic seaboard. By the mid-eighteenth century, large numbers of Scots and Scot-Irish also began to immigrate to the southern colonial region. Ethnic loyalties, kinship networks, and economic connections had always played an important role in constructing eighteenth-century communities. By chance, these newly arrived Scottish Highlanders, initially landing in the Carolinian and Georgian colonies, possessed strikingly similar cultural beliefs and practices with the indigenous Creek Indian population. These Creek-Scot similarities would help to create a common ground between the two cultures. An initial understanding and acceptance of each other's customs and values provided backcountry Scottish merchants with a valuable tool for creating social and economic trade alliances.[1]

The connections that were created between these Creek and Scottish individuals extended into the economic, political, and military spheres of influence. The primary tool used to create these trade networks was the institution of marriage, which provided a cohesive element between these two similar but separate ethnic groups. The practice of marriage between Scottish Indian traders and Creek Indian women was crucial in creating an *American mestizo* or *metis* class.

The term *American mestizo* is used in order to refer to the individuals who possess an ancestry that is Native American and European in origin. In the Southern backcountry, these relationships often were between Scottish or English male merchants and Creek, Choctaw, or Chickasaw women. Unfortunately, the only descriptive terms that exist in the American English language to describe the children produced from these relationships are "half-blood" or "mixed-breed". Both of these terms are disparaging and display a significant level of racial bias within the English language. In place of these expressions, the phrase *American mestizo* will be used since it is a far more linguistically neutral term.[2]

Many of these American mestizos became key players in the politics of the southeastern region. By the eighteenth century, these individuals, with their Creek and Scottish connections, would eventually dominate the social, economic, and political networks of

---

[1] Richard White, The Middle Ground: Indians, Empires, and Republics in the Great Lakes Region, 1650–1815 (Cambridge: Cambridge University Press, 1991), 50–93.

[2] William A. Haviland, Cultural Anthropology (New York: Harcourt Brace College Publishers, 1996), 31. For other authors who have used the term "American Mestizo" or its French equivalent "Metis," see Gary B. Nash, Red, White, and Black: The Peoples of Early America (Englewood Cliffs, New Jersey: Prentice - Hall, Inc, 1982), 278–279 and Richard White, The Middle Ground, 74.

the Southeastern backcountry. Alexander McGillivray's eventually political rise to power would emerge out of this environment.

McGillivray's future political influence was aided by the fact that Scottish Highlanders were able to successfully establish business/kinship connections with many of the Native Americans living in the Southeastern backcountry. Most of these "connections" were largely created and maintained through the practice of marriage. The predominate influence of specific Scottish families and clans in late seventeenth and early eighteenth-century Scotland, was transplanted to the American colonies. When these dominate families, such as the McGillivray's, realized that they could capitalized on these Scottish/Creek cultural parallels, some merchants used them in order to establish trade networks throughout the backcountry. Alexander's father, Lachlan McGillivray, capitalized on these accidental similarities and used them to his political advantage. Alexander McGillivray eventually inherited his father's social, political, and economic partnerships and alliances; and extended them far beyond Lachlan's original trade and kinship networks.

The patrilineal inheritance practices of the Scottish Highlanders combined well with the Creek Indian tradition of matrilineal inheritance, which gave Alexander McGillivray the full benefits of both cultural networks. As an American mestizo of Scottish and Creek ancestor, McGillivray had access to a vast array of kinship networks. His firmly established Creek ethnic traditions created a personal identity which was complemented by an Anglo-European education. Without this blending of Scottish influences into the complicated social matrix of Creek Indian society; McGillivray's ability to assume a coalescent-based role in the later years of his life would never have occurred. These Scottish and Creek influences were critical for the establishing of connections that would later greatly contribute to McGillivray's future achievements.[3]

.   .   .   .

The changes that were taking place within the Southern colonial region began long before Alexander McGillivray's birth and had become widespread, rapid, and permanent. The parade of European visitors to this region over the past centuries had left a permanent mark upon the indigenous populations. Strangers with bizarre customs, new and wonderful trade goods, as well as relentless diseases; created a varying array of cultural transitions and population shifts. If one is to fully understand the life and times of Alexander McGillivray, then one must examine the people and historical context of the greater region.

The initial exploration of the Southeast by the Spanish in the sixteenth century initiated a series of dramatic population shifts. The invasion of the Europeans, whether Spanish, French, or English, created an intermingling of cultures among the indigenous societies of the Southeast; as well as initiated an anthropologic process known as "acculturation". This meant that an environment was created in which an extensive borrowing of an invading cultures technology, values, and customs occurred. This "borrowing" was from the invading European societies with their advanced weaponry, disease, and numerous trade goods. By the time of Alexander McGillivray's birth, the colonial southern backcountry was a patchwork of mingling cultures, separate traditions, and ever-shifting trade networks.[4]

By 1750, the region of what is now present-day Alabama and western Georgia was the center of the Creek Confederacy. The

---

[3] Carol R. Ember & Melvin Ember, Cultural Anthropology (Englewood Cliffs, New Jersey: Prentice Hall, Inc, 1990), 33.

[4] John Walton Caughey, McGillivray of the Creeks (Norman: University of Oklahoma Press, 1959), 17; Ember & Ember, Cultural Anthropology, 355.

region in what is now the state of Mississippi was occupied by the Choctaws and Chickasaws tribes, who were considered distant ancestors of the Creek Indians. However, the Choctaw and Chickasaw Indians usually maintained a separate tribal identity and territory. The north, in the area that is now present-day Tennessee, was the ancestral homeland of the Cherokee Indian nation. To the south lay the Gulf of Mexico which was controlled by both the French and the Spanish monarchies, with their various outposts in the Caribbean, Louisiana, and Florida. During the seventeenth and eighteenth centuries, the eastern border of the Creek territory, in what is now present-day eastern Georgia and South Carolina; was becoming increasing populated by Anglo-European colonists and African slaves.[5]

The British colonies of North Carolina, South Carolina, and Georgia were rapidly growing in population, especially when compared to the neighboring Native American societies. Out of the many European social and ethnic groups that arrived in the American colonies, Scottish Highlanders created the deepest in-roads into the interior of the Southeast. Scottish Highlander men were far more successful at inter-marrying into, and trading with, the Creek Indians than the English, French, or Spanish. However, outside of the Creek Confederacy, the French and the Algonquin Indians had established similar marriage patterns and trade networks in the upper Midwest and Great Lakes region.[6]

In the eighteenth century, Scottish merchants who traveled into the Creek confederacy likely experienced and benefited from coincidental similarities between the Creek Indian's

---

[5] Caughey, McGillivray of the Creeks, 6; Carl Waldman, Atlas of the North American Indian (New York: Facts On File, Inc, 1985), 106; For a deeper understanding of African populations in the back country see, Peter Wood, Black Majority: Negroes in Colonial South Carolina from 1670 through the Stono Rebellion (New York: W. W. Norton & Company, 1974), 95-166.

[6] White, The Middle Ground, 50-93.

customs and Scottish Highlands traditions.[7]   The proof of this displayed in the fact that by 1750, Scottish Highlanders had started to monopolize European-Native American trade in the colonial southeast. At a minimum, by 1776, there were 150,000 Scots living in colonial America. Although there were many British traders in the southern backcountry, far more trading licenses bore Scottish surnames like McQueen, McGillivray, McIntosh, Campbell, and MacDonald.   Interestingly, most of this trade was controlled by members of the Scottish clan *Chattam,* of which the McGillivray Clan was a branch.[8]

The control of trade in the Southern backcountry, as well as Alexander McGillivray's eventual rise to prominence, was made possible because Scottish and Creek societies contained amazingly similar cultural parallels. For example, both Creeks and Scottish Highlanders were organized around and headed by protective chiefs who governed over various extended family groups or clans. In both Scot and Creek clan traditions, the position of this chief descended through family lineage. However, differences did arise in the area of gender relations, with Scottish colonist tracing their ancestry patrilineally; while Creek Indians adhered to matrilineal inheritance practices.[9] In other words, Scottish traditions vested

---

[7] Thomas John Kennedy,   "Origins of Creek Indian Nationalism: Contact, Diplomacy, Clans and Intermarriage During the Colonial and Early National Periods" (M.A. Thes., University of Houston, 1992), 89,91. William L. McDowell Jr. ed., Colonial Records of South Carolina: Documents relating to Indian Affairs, May 21, 1750-August 7, 1754 (Columbia: South Carolina Archives Department, 1958), 128 -129.

[8] Dorothy Downs, "British Influences on Creek and Seminole Men's Clothing, 1733-1858," Florida Anthropologist 33 (June 1980): 51. Ian Charles Cargill Graham, Colonist from Scotland: Emigration to North America, 1707-1783 (Port Washington, New York: Kennikat Press, 1972), 10-12. James Axtell also cites the same number (150,000), but for the entire eighteenth century; James Axtell, Beyond 1492: Encounters in Colonial America (Oxford: Oxford University Press, 1992), 227.

[9] T. C. Smout, A History the Scottish People 1560 - 1830 (St James Place, London: Collins, 1969), 39; Caughey, McGillivray of the Creeks, 13-16.

power and prestige in the father's side of the family, while Creek societies felt that status resided in the mother's ancestry.

The Creek Indian practice of tracing ancestral descent through the mother's lineage was not a totally foreign concept for Scottish immigrants. Occasionally, in Scottish highlander culture, the husband of the clan's female heiress assumed her name and the position of clan chief. Scot society, even though it was organized along patriarchal lines, provided women some legal protection and political power. Scottish Highlander women were held in high esteem and at various times in Scottish history wives were permitted to assist in council debates and settle disputes. These Scottish historical traditions were beneficial in allowing Scottish merchants in the backcountry to accept and work with the matriarchal traditions of Creek Indian society. [10]

Surprisingly, in manners of dress, the eighteenth-century Creek and Scottish Highlander societies also possessed coincidental similarities. Instead of the *trousers* or *breeches* that the English wore, the men in both societal groups wore a short, skirt-like dress. William Bartram, who traveled through the southeastern region in 1790, wrote that, "Sometimes [the Creek Indians wear] a flap, which covers their lower parts; this garment somewhat resembles the ancient Roman breeches, or the kilt of the Highlanders."[11] In addition, the very style and terminology for the footwear worn by Creek Indians and Scottish Highlanders was remarkably similar.

---

[10] Downs, "British Influences," 49. Robert Bain, The Clans and Tartans of Scotland Margaret O MacDougall ed. (London and Glasgow: Collins, 1968), 18.

[11] William Bartram, Travels in North & South Carolina, Georgia, (Philadelphia: 1792; reprint, Harrisonburg, Virginia: R. R. Donnelly & Sons Company, 1988), 500. Certain seventeenth and eighteenth century spellings have been corrected and changed to coincide with current English spelling rules. In most cases the letter "s" was inserted in place of the letter "f", with "fomewhat" becoming "somewhat" and "fet" becoming "set" These corrections were made to allow for a smoother reading of the primary quotes, while still maintaining much of the original writer's style.

The Algonquian term for a lightweight shoe made out of animal hide was "moccasin". Interestingly, the Gaelic term for a light and flexible shoe constructed out of soft animal hide was "mo casan".[12] John Lawson, during his 1701 trip through the Carolinas wrote that had, "Muster'd up another Pair of Shoes, or Moggisons," before setting out on his journey.[13] However, these chance similarities in clothing preferences between the Creeks and the Scots were only the beginning. Both societies shared additional similarities in regards to their cultural practices, beliefs, and traditions.

Both Highlanders and Creeks shared similar military traditions that glorified prowess on the battlefield. Historically, the introduction of English military technology had irreversibly altered both Scottish and Creek warfare. Both groups had formerly relied heavily upon the use of the bow and arrow. However, by the start of the eighteenth century, Creek Indians gained large scale access to black powder firearms. This access to weapons was achieved by participating in the international slave trade and filling the ever-expanding demand for slaves. By the end of the seventeenth century the Creeks were routinely attacking and kidnapping members of neighboring enemy tribes. English traders, out of the Carolinas, would sell Creek Indians firearms and gun powder in exchange for Native American slaves. Over time, however, the Creek Indians would become dependent upon trade with the Europeans in order to maintain their access to new weapon technology.[14]

Much like the Creek Indians, Scottish Highlanders had traditionally been excellent marksmen with the bow and arrow; but

---

[12] Downs, "British Influences," 50; John Telfar Dunbar, *History of Highland Dress* (Edinburgh: Oliver and Boyd, 1962), 164.

[13] John Lawson, *A New Voyage to Carolina* (London: 1709; reprint, Ann Arbor: University Microfilms, Inc, 1966), 41.

by the beginning of the eighteenth century firearms had replaced this traditional weapon.[15] Both cultures had experienced a shift in military weaponry largely due to the impact of English influences. However, the Scots and Creeks still maintained a style of fighting which resembled guerrilla warfare and usually emphasized close range combat.[16]

Creek and Scot warriors both used styles of combat that appeared in the eyes of the English to border on recklessness. Physical prowess, dramatic speeches, and courageous action during play and warfare were considered the ideal role models for male behavior.[17] Warfare was perceived, and used, as a tool for personal advancement in society and was actively pursued.[18] This predominance of military virtues in both cultures served McGillivray well during his rise to power in the years immediately following the American Revolution (1775-1783).

Additional analogous elements are apparent in the Creek Indian and Scottish Highlander belief and legal systems. For example, Creek Native American oaths were administered with a complexity comparable to the techniques employed in medieval "oathswearing".[19] Both Creeks and Highlanders shared close ties with nature, believed in supernatural spirits who inhabited the woods, and even consulted mystical oracles. Coincidentally, both

---

[14] David H. Corkran, The Creek Frontier, 1540 - 1783 (Norman: University of Oklahoma Press, 1967), 53.

[15] I. F. Grant, Periods in Highland History (London: Shepheard-Walwyn, 1987), 138; Bain, The Clans and Tartans of Scotland, 19.

[16] Kennedy, "Origins of Creek Indian Nationalism," 84.

[17] Downs, "British Influences," 49.

[18] L. G. Pine, The Highland Clans (Tokyo and Vermont: Charles E. Tuttle, Inc, 1972), 76; T. C. Smout, A History of the Scottish People, 46-47; John Phillip Reid, A Better Kind of Hatchet: Law, Trade, and Diplomacy in the Cherokee Nation during the Early Years of European Contact (University Park and London: Pennsylvania State University Press, 1976), 10.

[19] Harold J. Berman, Law and Revolution: The Formation of the Western Legal Tradition (Cambridge: Cambridge University Press, 1983), 58.

cultures possessed comparable rituals that celebrated dancing, feasting, and sacred fires.[20]

In regards to ethics, both groups believed that the ghost of a murdered family member was trapped on earth until his or her death had been revenged. For the Scots, justice for a victim's homicide did not hinge upon whether the specific agent responsible for the death was executed or severely punished. The most important factor was that someone from the guilty agent's family or clan died (paid a "bloodfine") in order to compensate for the death of the victim. In Creek Indian law, similar to the Scottish legal concept, justice for victims of homicide was based less upon retributive justice or deterrence and more upon compensation to those injured.[21]

In addition, Scottish Highlanders and Indian tribes of the colonial southeastern United States also possessed similar marriage practices. These martial traditions were related enough to create a degree of mutual understanding and potential compatibility. Marriage among many of the Creek Indian tribes was conducted in a more informal manner than that of the rigidly structured and piously-focused English marriages. Creek Indians considered marriage an agreement between two mutually consenting parties, which they celebrated with relatively simple and convenient ceremonies. One colonial observer noted in 1775 that the Creeks "marry without much ceremony, seldom any more than to make some presents to the parents, and to have a feast or hearty regale at the hut of the wife's Father." For Creek Indians in the eighteenth century, marriage and divorce was a simple proposition. A fact that is displayed by the existence of an

---

[20] Downs, "British Influences," 49.

[21] Kennedy, "Origins of Creek Indian Nationalism," 82; David Daiches ed., A Companion to Scottish Culture (New York: Holmes & Meier Publishers, Inc, 1981), 38; Rennard Strickland, Fire and

abbreviated, informal marriage ceremony, called the "Toopsa Tawah" (make-haste-wedding).[22]

In Scotland, marriage was more compatible with the Creek institution than in many other parts of Europe during this time. The Reformation in Scotland had made marriage a legal contract between two people and not an unbreakable religious bond. The implications of this meant that divorce was legally possible. After the Reformation, marriage in Scotland had become less formal as opposed to the practices and procedures of neighboring England. In Scotland, a church marriage was still considered the regular practice, but a number of other irregular forms of marriage had become legally acceptable.

For example, the first irregular form of Scottish marriage was "by habit and repute", that is co-habitation which was accepted as a legal marital union. The second irregular form of marriage was by declaration "de praesenti", which meant a declaration before witness. The third was marriage by promise subsequenti copula, which meant after sex relations. And yet another custom of Scottish clan society, known as "handfasting", allowed couples to live together for an announced period of time. If problems arose during the co-habitation, either party possessed the ability to dissolve the relationship. The development and establishment of these flexible views of marriage as a binding agreement between two consenting parties in Scotland made Creek Indian marital customs more acceptable to eighteenth-century Scots.[23]

Even the physical punishment for certain crimes in the Creek Confederacy would have appeared familiar to Scottish

---

the Spirits: Cherokee Law from Clan to Court (Norman: University of Oklahoma Press, 1975), 27.

[22] Bernard Romans, A Concise Natural History of East and West Florida (1775; reprint, Gainesville: University of Florida Press, 1962), 97; Caughey, McGillivray of the Creeks, 12.

[23] Daiches, ed., A Companion to Scottish Culture, 240-241; Bain, Clans and Tartans of Scotland, 18.

Highlanders witnessing these practices. For example, the penalties for marital infidelity were shockingly similar, if not nearly identical, in both cultures. Individuals found guilty of adultery were commonly punished by body deformity. Numerous first-hand accounts from the southeastern Indian tribes describe a punishment which entailed cutting the guilty party's ears off.[24] One late eighteenth-century traveler recorded that a Creek Indian chief, believing his wife had committed infidelity with a trader, "resolved to exact legal satisfaction, which in this case is cutting off both ears of the delinquent, close to the head, which is called cropping."[25] Colonel Benjamin Hawkins, one of the first United States Indian Affairs agents, mentions in 1798 that the Creek Indians' customary punishment for adultery was to, "beat them severely with sticks, and then crop them."[26] Again, out of sheer coincidence, in Scottish traditions individuals who were found guilty of sexual infraction had their ears cut off through a similarly brutal process called "lugging."[27]

     .   .   .   .

Unexpected cultural similarities between Creek Indians and Scottish immigrants undoubtedly help to facilitate a high number of cross-cultural marriages. Most of the Scots who were transported to America were men without financial assets. Marriage to well-positioned Native American women was a natural conclusion if one was seeking and economic advantage in the Southeastern backcountry is particularly true since Indians were the dominant force politically, militarily, and economically in the

---

[24] Rennard Strickland, <u>Fire and the Spirits</u>, 170; Caughey, <u>McGillivray of the Creeks</u>, 12; also see , James Adair, <u>History of the American Indians</u>, Samuel Cole Williams ed., (London: Edward and Charles Dilly, 1775, reprint; New York: Argonaut Press, 1974), 152.

[25] Bartram, <u>Travels in North America</u>, 446.

[26] Benjamin Hawkins, <u>A Sketch of the Creek Country</u> (New York: Kraus Reprint Company, 1971), 74.

[27] I. F. Grant, <u>Periods in Highland History</u>, 150.

Southeast. John Lawson, who explored South Carolina at the start of the eighteenth century, illustrates this point clearly when he states that unless a backcountry trader married into the Native American culture, "tis impossible for him ever to accomplish his Designs amongst that People."[28]

One of the myths in American history is the belief that, outside of New Spain (Latin America) and New France (Canada) there was little intermarriage between Native Americans and Europeans, but surviving statements made by eighteenth-century witnesses cast an illuminating light on this pervasive practice. In 1737, a Mr. Tanner who had resided among the Creeks noted that, "all the Indian Traders have wives among the Indians, being necessary for dressing their victuals, and carrying on their business; there were 400 children so begotten."[29]

Interestingly, the Earl of Egmont commented that, "the Indians are extremely human to those in friendship with them, perfectly just in their dealings, & know not what it is to tell a lie."[30] The key term from this quote is the word "friendship". If the best method of obtaining business connections with Native Americans was through the construction "friendships" for beneficial "dealings" -- the most convenient way to create and maintain those friendships was through marriage into Native American society.[31]   These connections to the numerous Creek kinship networks provided

---

[28] Lawson, _A New voyage to Carolina_, 185; J. Leitch Wright, Jr., _The Only Land They Knew: The Tragic Story of the American Indians in the Old South_ (New York: The Free Press, 1981), 234.

[29] Robert G. McPherson ed., _The Journal of the Earl of Egmont: Abstract for Establishing the Colony of Georgia, 1732-1738_ (Athens: University of Georgia Press, 1962), 272-273.

[30] McPherson, ed., _Journal of the Earl of Egmont_, 272.

[31] Gary B. Nash, "The Image of the Indian in the Southern Colonial Mind," _William and Mary Quarterly_ 29 (April, 1972): 222.

irreplaceable business tools for merchants in the southern backcountry.[32]

While it strengthened economic networks, intermarriage sometimes created ambiguity and confusion about the cultural identity of the children produced from these unions. Records state that southeastern mestizo children were "left and bred up by their mothers." As a result, "they speak both Indian & English, So that there are now few Indians that do not Speak English enough to be understood: but whatever is the reason, they do not care to do it but when drunk."[33] Overall, the majority of southern colonists of European descent did not consider these bilingual mestizos to be European in ancestry, but instead perceived them as possessing the same racial identity as a Native American.

Interestingly, the fact that American mestizos would speak English only when sufficiently intoxicated suggests that they felt an uneasiness, or even animosity, toward Anglo-American culture. These multiracial individuals, who felt rejected or scorned by their father's European culture, likely perceived English to be an insult to their pride and personal identity. Yet, these American mestizos, who were members of the Creek Confederacy, were accustomed to political and economic dominance within Creek society. There is a chance that the increased competition from an ever-expanding number of European/American colonists likely created resentment among these individuals, with the distastefulness of speaking their fathers' language only overcome by the loosening of social inhibitions through alcohol.

In the eighteenth century, one could not escape the racial attitudes of the average European colonist, particularly the

---

[32] Marriage was not the only type of cross-cultural relations. Slavery or forced marriage was also used. Daniel H. Usner Jr., Indians, settlers, & Slaves in a Frontier Exchange Economy (Chapel Hill: University of North Carolina Press: Chapel Hill, 1992), 57.

English. During this same time period, there was a dramatic increase in the use of Africans as slaves; which meant that social position, skin color, and physical characteristics (race) were increasingly seen as more directly affecting ones standing in society. In other words, by the mid-eighteenth century, a darker skin tone was seen as a mark of inferiority to the average European colonists in both North and South America.

Alexander belonged to this new group of American mestizo children whose cultural identity was, at times, ambiguous. However, his dual cultural heritage also furnished the connections and opportunities he needed to maneuver within the politically complex world of the southeastern region. To understand how the blending of Highland Scot and Creek traditions influenced his development, one must first examine the background of his parents, Lachlan McGillivray and Sehoy of the Koasati (Creek Wind Clan).

·   ·   ·   ·

The life of Lachlan McGillivray is fascinating on its own account, yet some scholars have ignored his activities; choosing instead to focus on his son's achievements. This is unfortunate due to the fact that Lachlan McGillivray was an influential person in the region during his lifetime. However, a few scholars have explored Lachlan's personal history, which largely took place in the southern British colonies of Georgia and South Carolina as well as in the confines of the Creek Confederacy.

Lachlan McGillivray was 16 or 17 years old when he first arrived in the southern colonies, and immediately pursued a career as a backcountry Indian merchant.[34] The tradition historical

---

33 McPherson, ed., Journal of the Earl of Egmont, 273.

34 E. Merton Coulter and Albert B. Saye ed., A List of the Early Settlers of Georgia (Athens: University of Georgia Press, 1949), 83-84; Michael D. Green, "Alexander McGillivray," Studies in Diversity: American Indian Leaders, ed. R. David Edmunds (Lincoln and London: University of Nebraska Press, 1980), 42; Edward J. Cashin, Lachlan McGillivray, Indian Trader: The Shaping

account correctly describes him as the son of wealthy parents from Dunmaglass, Scotland. The accuracy and truthfulness of the rest of his early years, however, have been distorted by romance and myth. Early historians claimed that Lachlan ran away from his childhood home in Scotland at the age of 16 to seek adventure, and that he sailed into the Charlestown harbor in the mid-1730s. Lachlan is reported to have arrived in the colony with only a shilling in his pocket and the clothes he wore, yet he was able to amass a considerable fortune in a few decades since he possessed, "an honest heart, a fearless disposition, and cheerful spirits which seldom became depressed."[35]

The traditional historical account continues by stating that the young Lachlan joined a band of backcountry Carolina traders, who paid the newly arrived immigrant with a jack knife. The ambitious Scotsman supposedly traded the knife with a neighboring Indian tribe for an undocumented quantity of deerskin pelts, which were then bartered for profit in Charlestown.[36] Lachlan quickly assumed a career as a colonial trader, eventually establishing a trading post in the region of the abandoned French settlement of Fort Toulouse.[37] His post was located at the confluence of the Coosa and Tallapoosa Rivers (present-day Alabama) in the center of what was considered the Creek nation.[38] Romanticized accounts of Lachlan's early years fail to mention critical historical elements that were necessary for the establishment of his, and ultimately Alexander's, career.

---

of the Southern Colonial Frontier (Athens: University of Georgia Press, 1992).

[35] Albert J. Pickett, History of Alabama and Incidentally of Georgia and Mississippi From the Earliest Period (Charleston: Walker and James, 1851; reprint, Birmingham, Alabama: Birmingham Book and Magazine Co., 1962), 342.

[36] Ibid, 342-343.

[37] This outpost was established four hundred miles upstream from the French settlement at Mobile primarily to control the Indian trade of the region. Caughey, McGillivray of the Creeks, 11.

[38] Pickett, History of Alabama, 343.

Many early accounts fail to mention that the McGillivray Family possessed a rich tradition of leadership and influence in Scotland. As a child, Lachlan lived in the mansion house of Dunmaglass in the river valley of the Nairn. His grandfather, Farquhar McGillivray, had built this mansion and was a former chief of the Clan McGillivray. The young Lachlan was raised by his parents, William and Janet, and had a sister named Jean as well as a younger brother named Alexander. In 1685 Farquhar was rewarded for his loyalty to the Stuart Monarchy with a government position of commissioner of supplies. However, Farquhar died in 1714, just one year before the political turmoil created by James Stuart the Pretender in 1715.[39]

Grandfather Farquhar's sons were devoted Jacobites and rallied many of the Scottish clans in support of the Stuart Monarchy. Lachlan's oldest uncle Farquhar II (the seventh clan chief) served as a captain in the Jacobite army, while his father, William, was a lieutenant. During the 1715 Scottish uprising, the Jacobite leader chose to surrender rather than fight. During this surrender, sixteen McGillivrays were among the captured Jacobite prisoners. Soon afterwards, thirteen of these captives were deported to the British colony of South Carolina, where they created a new branch of the McGillivray Clan. Among the existing public records of the deported McGillivray Highlanders there were numerous names, such as Archibald, John, and an older Lachlan McGillivray, with all of above individuals having a direct influence upon the history of early colonial South Carolina.[40]

The earlier exploits of the McGillivrays was an important contribution to the success of Alexander's father within the colonial

---

[39] Cashin, Lachlan McGillivray, 6-7.
[40] The McGillivray clan also made a name for itself in the fight for Charles Edward in 1745. The historian Thomas Macaulay wrote that King George and the royal court were alarmed at the invasion

Southeast. The early migration of McGillivray clan members created a strong foundation of kinship networks. Farquhar II, the chief, and his younger brother William (Lachlan's father) escaped deportation and returned to Strathnairn with enhanced reputations as individuals who had been tested in battle. Shortly after, William established his home in the ancestral seat of his McGillivray Clan, Dunmaglass. William McGillivray married Janet McIntosh of Kyllachy on February 9, 1714, with Lachlan being born in 1719.[41]

Even before his birth, Lachlan was assured of a fairly prosperous childhood at Dunmaglass, since his father's estate in the valley of the Nairn River was the most honored and favored site of the Clan McGillivray. The additional kinship connection between the McGillivrays and the McIntoshes also played a contributing role in Lachlan's success in colonial North America. The fact that Alexander McGillivray's patriarchal grandmother was a member of the McIntosh clan increased his personal influence. Decades after Alexander McGillivray's death in 1793, another American mestizo named William McIntosh (1778-1825) assumed a similar Creek leadership position. The career of the Creek Indian leader William McIntosh displayed the lingering traces of earlier Scot/Creek alliances.

According to colonial records, Lachlan McGillivray embarked for Georgia on October 20, 1735 and arrived the following January, listed as a "servant" to Jo Mackintosh.[42] The Lachlan's mother was a McIntosh which meant that the young Scot likely traveled to the colonies with an extended member of his clan. In fact, Kinship-based connections provided "natural communities" for many European immigrants in the colonies. Basic kinship

---

of 1745 as if "the wild Macgillivrays were even then plundering in the Strand." Ibid, 7.

[41] Benjamin W. Griffith Jr., McIntosh and Weatherford, Creek Indian leaders (Tuscaloosa: University of Alabama Press, 1988), xi-xiii, 1-11.

connections were established in New England, the Middle colonies, and as well as the South.[43]

Lachlan, undoubtedly, was aided by the respectability of his family name which provided a "stepping stone" which assisted in the construction of substantial trade networks throughout the Southeast. Political and economic connections were easier to achieve, since members of the McGillivray clan already resided in the Carolina and Georgia colonies. Alexander's father may have possessed "an honest heart" and "a fearless disposition" but having relatives in beneficial positions was a supporting factor in his eventually financial success that should not be overlooked.

Lachlan expanded his opportunities for success when he married Sehoy, a Creek Indian woman from the Wind Clan (Koasati). The historical information about Alexander's mother, Sehoy, is limited and perplexing. The debate over the correct ethnic background of Alexander McGillivray's mother displays the sheer complexity of the southeastern region in the eighteenth century. Some scholars argue that Sehoy's father was French (Marchand?), while others believe that he was a Native American.[44] Spanish documents from 1783 suggest a Native American ancestry

---

[42] Coulter and Saye ed., A List of the Early Settlers, 83-84.

[43] Many of the individuals involved in the Indian trade belonged to the Clan Chattam, which bound them in a network which contemporaries understood but historians rarely recognize. Cashin, Lachlan McGillivray, 57; Fussell Chalker, "Highlands Scots in the Georgia Lowlands," Georgia Historical Quarterly LX (Spring 1976): 36; Bernard Bailyn, The Peopling of British North America: An Introduction (New York: Vintage Books, 1988), 55.

[44] Thomas Foreman argues in "Alexander McGillivray," Chronicles of Oklahoma 8 (March, 1929), 107, that Sehoy's mother was a Creek woman, while her father was a French man named Captain Marchand. Marchand was supposedly stationed at Fort Toulouse where he was killed during a mutiny in 1722. The earliest record of Captain Marchand as Sehoy's father is in Albert James Pickett's, History of Alabama, 342-343. Mary Ann Oglesby Neeley's, "Lachlan McGillivray: Scot on the Alabama Frontier," Alabama Historical Quarterly (Spring: 1974), 7, draws a different conclusion. She cites Thomas Woodward's Reminiscences of the Creek or Muskoghe Indians (Mobile: Southern University Press, 1865), 52-54, which argues that Sehoy was a full-blood Creek Indian. Woodward and Neeley both state that there never was a Captain Marchand

with Arturo O' Neill, a Spanish officer who was well acquainted with Alexander McGillivray, writing to the Governor of Havana that, "the middle of last month there arrived here Alexander Maguilberi, half-breed son of a Scotchman and an Indian woman of the Wind Clan, a sister of the Indian chief named Red Shoes."[45]

Furthermore, both Lachlan and Alexander's writings never made any mention of French ancestry. It is possible that nineteenth-century scholars, consciously or unconsciously, increased Alexander McGillivray's European ethnicity so that his feats were easier to accept. A French grandfather would have meant that Alexander was *culturally*, more European than Native American. A significant number of scholars from the nineteenth (and even the twentieth) century, viewed Native American populations as idiotic, savage, and uncivilized individuals who would have been hard pressed to produce a person with the political skill of Alexander McGillivray. The more "European" he was made, the easier it was to comprehend and compartmentalize his diplomatic achievements.

The fact that matriarchal lines of inheritance were stressed in Creek society ultimately makes the ethnic identity of Sehoy's father less important.[46] Of much greater significance was her membership in the influential Wind Clan. The Creek Indians, by the mid-eighteenth century, had evolved into two separate sub-Creek cultures, the Lower Creeks and the Upper Creeks; with Alexander McGillivray and his mother's Wind Clan residing within

---

serving as commander at Fort Toulouse. For further reading on Sehoy and this debate see, Cashin, Lachlan McGillivray, 71-74.

[45] *O'Neill* to *Ezpeleta*, October 19, 1783, Caughey, McGillivray of the Creeks, 62; John C. Fitzpatrick, editor of George Washington's manuscript sources, also does not mention the French ancestry of Alexander's mother, stating that he was the son of a loyalist and "a Creek woman." John C. Fitzpatrick, The Writings of George Washington vol. 30 (Washington: United States Government Printing Office, 1939), 379.

[46] For the role of American Indian women in encounters between Europeans and Indians in the New World see, Clara Sue Kidwell,

the territory of the Upper Creeks. During this time period the Creek Confederacy included as many as fifty distinct clans, much in the same tradition as the Highland Scots' clan system. Out of these numerous clans, each with its own identity, seven to ten clans dominated Creek tribal politics. It is interesting to note that members from the Wind Clan occupied the greatest percentage of the high-ranking civil government positions.[47]

The Creek Confederacy following the American Revolution, consisted of roughly fifty-two villages, with a Wind Clan member likely present either as a town chief or council member in most of the Confederacy's villages. However, the number of actual Creek villages probably varied due to the creation and destruction of alliances made with peripheral towns of the Choctaw, Chickasaw, and Cherokee tribes.[48]

Before marrying Lachlan McGillivray, the Creek Native Sehoy bore a daughter with Malcolm McPherson. It appears beyond the possibility of sheer coincidence that it was also Malcolm McPherson who first introduced Lachlan to the backcountry Indian trade.[49] In fact, the name McPherson was an extended branch of the dominant Clan Chattam.[50] Lachlan's marriage with Sehoy

---

"Indian Women as Cultural Mediators," Ethnohistory 39 (Spring 1992): 97.

[47] J. Leitch Wright Jr., Creeks & Seminoles: The Destruction and Regeneration of the Muscogulge People (Lincoln: University of Nebraska Press, 1986), 3; Verner W. Crane, "The Origins of the Name of the Creek Indians," Mississippi Valley Historical Review 5 (December 1918): 339-342; Green, "Alexander McGillivray," 42-43.

[48] Major Celeb Swan, "Position and State of Manners and Arts in the Creek, or Muscogee Nation in 1791," 1795, in Henry Rowe Schoolcraft, Historical and Statistical Information respecting the History, Conditions, and Prospects of the Indian Tribes of the United States vol. 5 (Philadelphia: Lippincott, Grambo, & Company, 1851-57), 26; John R. Swanton, Early History of the Creek Indians and Their Neighbors (Washington: United States Government Printing Office, 1922), Map attached to inside of book's back flap cover.

[49] Neeley, "Lachlan McGillivray," 7.

[50] Cashin, Lachlan McGillivray, 74.

coincided nicely with the rapidly expanding network of Creek and Scottish trade relationships.

Lachlan and Sehoy gradually developed a prosperous business, based on trade with the Native Americans. The Scottish immigrant even became a proficient interpreter, with Lachlan demonstrating his multi-lingual abilities during treaty negotiations between the Creeks and the colonial government of South Carolina. In 1756 the South Carolina governor wrote to a Creek chief stating that he, "desired Mr. McGillivray who is well skilled in your language to wait on you, and who being the Interpreter I made use of upon this Occasion, will explain whatever may seem obscure"[51]

Lachlan McGillivray utilized his Native American trade connections to his advantage. By 1762, Lachlan was a substantial land owner near the town of Savannah, Georgia, and was eventually elected captain of the coastal town's militia. During the following years he held a seat in the Assembly representing the Christ Church Parish and served as a justice of the peace. In fact, one of the most detailed first-hand accounts of eighteenth-century Indian tribes (1775) in the Southeast is actually dedicated to Lachlan McGillivray. The man who had once been a lowly backcountry Indian trader was now a respected member of Georgia's new gentry class.[52]

.   .   .   .

By the time of Alexander McGillivray's birth, his parents were well-established in both the Creek Confederacy and Southern Colonial Society. Their positions of prominence in two separate cultures shaped the young child's future in important ways. During his childhood, Alexander learned how to live as both a Creek Indian

---

[51] *Governor Glenn* [James] to *Malatchi* [Mico], January 31, 1756, McDowell ed., Documents Relating to Indian Affairs, 91.
[52] Cashin, Lachlan McGillivray, 255-256. James Adair, History of the American Indians Samuel Cole Williams ed. (London: Edward

and a European-American. Alexander himself was named by his father after a Scottish chief who was considered a hero and had died at the head of his clan at Culloden.[53] Historians have disagreed over the correct date of Alexander McGillivray's birth, citing dates ranging from 1739 to 1759.[54] However, in his final will Lachlan states that Alexander McGillivray was born on December 15, 1750.[55] The 1750 date is feasible because a birth date on this year would have allowed the young McGillivray to participate in the American Revolution while still in his late twenties. Earlier dates of birth are possible, but a 1759 date creates a much younger historical figure that would have only been 16 years old at the start Revolution in 1775.

Lachlan and Sehoy created a home near the bank of the Little Tallassee River, which was only a few miles upstream from the Coosa River (present day Alabama) within the territory of the Creek Confederacy. Alexander, along with his two sisters Jeannet and Sophia, spent his first years on the Little Tallassee plantation.[56] His early childhood and adolescent experiences provide valuable insight into his personal cultural identity. The cultural duality of Alexander's early life experiences perhaps help to explain the motivations behind the decisions that he made later in life. One must remember that the young McGillivray's childhood was most likely dominated by his mother's Creek culture.

---

and Charles Dilly, 1775; reprint, New York: Argonaut Press, 1974), xxxiii.

[53] Cashin, Lachlan McGillivray, 73.

[54] Albert Pickett in his History of Alabama, 345, claims that Alexander was thirty years old in 1778, which meant that he was born in 1748. The historian Samual Drake (1841) records that 1739 was his birth date; Cashin, Lachlan McGillivray, 333. Contemporary historian Michael Green, cites John W. Caughey's date of 1759 from McGillivray of the Creeks, as the most likely date of birth Alexander McGillivray.

[55] Lachlan McGillivray's will, June 12, 1767, State of Alabama Department of Archives and History, Montgomery, Alabama.

[56] Mary Ann Oglesby Neeley, "Lachlan McGillivray: A Scot on the Alabama Frontier," Alabama Historical Quarterly 36 (Spring, 1974), 8.

John Lawson records in 1709, with a tone of disgust, that when Anglo-American men and Indian women produced children, "all the children go along with the Mother, and none with the Father. And therefore, on this Score [sic], it ever seems impossible for the Christians to get their Children (which they have by these *Indian* Women) away from them; whereby they might bring them up in the Knowledge of the Christian Principles."[57]

The Creek practice of matriarchal authority during childhood would have helped to promote a very powerful "Creek" identity in the young Alexander. This Creek Indian cultural identity likely continued throughout his life. Although the son of an influential Highland Scot, the first cultural traits he was exposed to was Native American.[58] McGillivray's future political and diplomatic dealings displayed a dynamic and fluid view of the world, but his core identity was always pro-Creek Indian.[59]

Although Creek practices and customs demanded that the mother raise the children, this did not mean that Creek children had no male role model during their formative years. Creek childrearing practices had the maternal uncle, or *tawa,* provide the necessary masculine influence to a child's early socialization. The evidence that survives concerning Alexander's childhood suggests that he was raised under Sehoy's supervision, with Lachlan only allowed a modest influence.[60] During Alexander's early years Lachlan lived either with, or in close proximity, to his son.[61] The

---

[57] John Lawson, A New Voyage to Carolina, 185.

[58] For recent interpretations of psychological development in early childhood see: Wayne Weiten, Psychology: Themes and Variations (Pacific Grove, California: Brooks/Cole Publishing Company, 1992), 388, 403; Henry Gleitman, Psychology (New York: W.W. Norton & Company, 1991), 588.

[59] For a discussion of the relationship between cultural identity, personal history, and physical space see: Xiao-Lun Wang, "Cultural Mediators or Marginal Persons?" Geographical Review 81 (July, 1991): 292.

[60] Caughey, McGillivray of the Creeks, 13.

[61] Cashin, Lachlan McGillivray, 79.

belief that Lachlan lived with, or had contact with, Alexander as a child is based upon educated speculations. The fact that Alexander McGillivray was proficient with the English language, both written and oral, implies that an Anglo-American influence was present during his childhood and adolescence years. However, Lachlan's influence on Alexander was not evident until the later years of his son's adolescence.

If Alexander's early childhood even remotely resembled Creek tribal customs, his maternal uncle would have possessed more input into the boy's socialization than his father. Alexander's maternal uncle was a famous Upper Creek war chief named Red Shoes, who was also a member of the Wind clan and one of the six most powerful leaders in the Creek Confederacy.[62] The overall influence of Red Shoes upon his nephew's worldview is not fully known, but a surviving letter from McGillivray does mention his uncle's death. "Your Excellency was pleased to send me [an account] of the death of my relation old Red Shoes, for whose loss I am real[l]y sorry, as he has been always a faithfull & Couragious Leader."[63]

Although Red Shoes, rather than Lachlan, may have dominated Alexander's earliest education; the two men likely held many traits in common.[64] Both Scottish and Creek clans possessed rich family histories of battle, as well as firm leadership traditions within their respected societies. The young McGillivray possessed strong military role models on both sides of his family. Perhaps, the compatibility of Creek and Highland Scottish cultures created a

---

[62] Green, "Alexander McGillivray," 42; *O'Neill* to *Miro*, February 17, 1784, Caughey, McGillivray of the Creeks, 71-72.

[63] *McGillivray* to *O'Neill*, January 3, 1784, Caughey, McGillivray of the Creeks, 66.

[64] Alexander's uncle Red Shoes should not be confused with the Choctaw chief (Shulush Houma) of the same name who was assassinated in June of 1747. Usner, Indians, Settlers, & Slaves, 88, 92-93; There was also an old Cowassada chieftain named Red Shoes who lived in 1793. Swanton, Early History of the Creek Indians, 204.

unified heritage rather than conflicting traditions. These family traditions of military leadership that were stressed during Alexander's formative years would continue to influence him throughout his adult life.

The full extent of Alexander's European education is vague and largely lost to history. Since the young boy resided in the Creek Confederacy during his early years, Lachlan likely hired tutors to travel to the Confederacy in order to teach his first born son. However, logic dictates that any outside tutoring would have remained within the confines of Creek child-rearing practices.[65]

During Alexander's adolescent years, his schooling was continued in Charlestown where he received a classic eighteenth-century education. His learning was supplemented in 1767 by working as a clerk under Samuel Elbert, a prominent Savannah merchant and future colonel for the Georgia militia during the American Revolution.[66] Besides Elbert, Alexander also completed an apprenticeship with the Savannah-based firm of Inglis, Hall, and Company.[67]

Historians are unsure as to what was the full extent, and exact nature, of Alexander's education during his residence in Charlestown and Savannah. Some researchers claim that the young Alexander was also tutored by his cousin Farquhar

---

[65] For information on Creek Indian child rising practices see, John R. Swanton, Social Organization and Social Usage's of the Indians of the Creek Confederacy (Washington: United States Government Printing Office, 1924), 363-367; Caughey, McGillivray of the Creeks, 13-15.

[66] Kenneth Coleman ed., A History of Georgia (Athens: University of Georgia Press, 1977), 78; Robert S. Davis Jr., Georgia Citizens and Soldiers of the American Revolution (Easley, South Carolina: Southern Historical Press, Inc., 1979), 116.

[67] In 1841 Samuel Drake named Alexander McGillivray's tutors in Charlestown as Mr. Sheed and William Henderson. Henderson taught Latin and later achieved some prominence as a literary critic in London. George Sheed was the writing master at the Charlestown free school, with William Henderson was the Latin teacher in charge of the free school from 1753 to 1763. Cashin, Lachlan McGillivray, 75; In 1767 Alexander is mentioned as still employed as an "apprentice to Messrs Inglis and Hall." Lachlan

McGillivray, a minister in the Presbyterian Church.[68] It is clear that Alexander's education provided him with a mastery of the English language, which was clearly evident in his correspondences. People who had visited Alexander, and later described him, commonly referred to his "educated" intellect. A visitor to his plantation in 1791 noted that Alexander "possesses an Atticism of Diction aided by a liberal Education."[69] Some historians claim that during his apprenticeship in Savannah the young McGillivray spent most of his spare time, and part of his employers, reading books on European history. Other historical references of Alexander described his intellect as "well acquainted with all the most useful European sciences."[70]

•   •   •   •

By the time he was an adult, Alexander McGillivray was economically and politically well-positioned in the eighteenth-century southeastern region. His multi-ethnic cultural heritage allowed him to benefit from the economic connections of his father, while at the same time inheriting his mother's political connections. If Alexander was raised according to traditional Creek Indian customs, his mother and uncle would have possessed a tremendous influence on his childhood development. Pre-existing similarities

---

McGillivray's will, June 12, 1767, State of Alabama Department of Archives and History, Montgomery, Alabama.

[68] Caughey, McGillivray of the Creeks, 15. Cashin explores this claim, but could find no record of a McGillivray in the Scots Church Records; Cashin, Lachlan McGillivray, 74. Documents from 1753 describe Farquhar McGillivray as a cabinetmaker living in Charlestown; Caroline T. Moore ed., Abstracts of the Wills of the State of South Carolina, 1740-1760 (Columbia: R. L. Bryan, 1964), 164.

[69] John Pope, A Tour Through the Southern and Western Territories of the United States of North America: The Spanish Dominions on the River Mississippi, and the Floridas: The Countries of the Creek Nations; and Many Unhabited Parts, (Richmond: John Dixion, 1792, reprint; Gainesville: University of Florida Press, 1979), 48.

[70] Obituary Notice in The Gentleman's Magazine, "Marriages and Deaths of considerable Persons," August, 1793, (London), Vol. LXIII, part II, 767, reprint in Caughey, McGillivray of the Creeks, 362; Marian F. Morse, "Alexander McGillivray: Who put

between Creek Indian and Scottish highlander culture likely meant that these two cultures reinforced Alexander's Creek childhood identity. During his adolescent years, he received a European-style education and apprenticeships in the southern British colonies. These experiences, as well as the young American mestizo's dual cultural heritage and inherited kinship networks, ultimately placed him in an advantageous situation.[71] The worldview that Alexander had likely developed by the start of the American Revolution was complex and encompassing, due to his unique cultural background.

---

not his trust in Princes," (M.A. Thes., Florida State College for Women, 1936) 4.

[71] Cashin, Lachlan McGillivray, 77.

Chapter 2

♦

The Interpreter: 1775 - 1784

Alexander McGillivray, as a British military officer and Creek Indian leader, did not always fit the historically established stereotypes associated with these roles. The trials of the American Revolution provided McGillivray with valuable training experience. These experiences within the field of military diplomacy and international politics aided him in developing his leadership abilities and credentials as a Native American leader.

By the 1776, southern Native American societies were increasingly feeling the effects of European and American pressures, with attempts to maintain a neutral stance between these colonial powers eventually failing. The aggressive position taken by many of the colonists during, and after, the American Revolution forced Alexander, as well as many other Native Americans, to seek military and diplomatic support from the European monarchies. The McGillivray family had sided with the British and loyalist cause during the revolution, which meant that with an American victory led to the loss of their family's estate and possessions. This large financial loss combined with loyalist beliefs and sympathies, likely encouraged an anti-American sentiment among both Alexander and his allies.

His connection to an extensive trade network, intellectual abilities, as well as pro-loyalist position, allowed Alexander to become a commissioned officer in the British Army. Alexander originally assumed a commissary role for the British, but quickly expanded his influence beyond this formal title. He would also assume the role of interpreter, becoming a diplomatic mediator between the Creek nation and the British government. His military actions displayed the rationale of an individual whose cultural identity was firmly Creek Indian, while simultaneously possessing a thorough understanding of British colonial society and international diplomacy. McGillivray's connections to the Creek towns and their war chiefs provided a stable base of influence which, by 1783, had started to draw the attention of the Spanish government. A letter written by a Spanish official who was in close contact with Alexander McGillivray and was the acting captain general in Havana, Cuba stated that "the said Maguilberi, I am well informed, has more influence among the Creek Nations than any other person; therefore, and because he was educated at Charleston, the English named him commissary for the Upper Creek Nations."[1]

·   ·   ·   ·

Some historians have circulated the idea that McGillivray "was no warrior" but instead, "lived in comfort and safety at his plantations on the Coosa while the Indians did his fighting."[2] In fact, McGillivray led war parties and did not simply reside at his plantation during the Revolutionary War period. He was active in the American Revolution and helped raise Creek detachments in order to help the British military defend Pensacola. On two separate occasions he marched Creek warriors to aid the British General John Campbell's defense of Pensacola, even leading a war party which possessed six hundred members. During another field

---

[1] *O'Neill to Ezpeleta*, October 19, 1783, John Walton Caughey, McGillivray of the Creeks (Norman: University of Oklahoma Press, 1959), 62.

[2] Arthur Preston Whitaker, "Alexander McGillivray, 1783-1789," North Carolina Historical Review 5 (April 1928): 184-185.

campaign, McGillivray's war party was ambushed by American Rebels, which resulted in the loss of six Creek warriors due to casualties.

Interestingly, a William McIntosh was one of the British deputy commissary officers for the Lower Creeks. One should remember that Alexander McGillivray's paternal grandmother was a member of the McIntosh Clan (Janet McIntosh). This same William McIntosh was likely a distant relative of Alexander McGillivray, a direct legacy of the Scottish/Creek trade and diplomatic relationships that existed in the Southeast.[3]

As a British war agent, McGillivray uncovered an American plot in 1777 that had attempted to expel loyalist traders from the Creek towns, as well as assassinate two British Indian agents. The two targeted British agents were saved only because McGillivray learned of the conspiracy and promptly warned them. The agents, as well as numerous British Indian traders, were forced to flee to Pensacola for a short time until tensions eased.[4] With accomplishments of this nature, why did some historians portrayed Alexander McGillivray in a non-warrior manner?

A likely reason for this description was the fact that McGillivray was not blessed with robust physical health. Sources from the time period state that "he was often so weakened that he could not mount a horse, so stiffened by rheumatism that he could not grasp a quill, so racked by pain that he could not enter into conversation."[5] Those who knew McGillivray described him as possessing "a Constitution originally delicate and feeble. ·· He is

---

[3] James H. O'Donnell, "Alexander McGillivray, Training for Leadership, 1777-1783," Georgia Historical Quarterly 49 (June, 1965): 177-180; For a further discussion of Alexander McGillivray's leadership of war parties see, J. Leitch Wright, Anglo-Spanish Rivalry in North America (Athens: University of Georgia Press, 1971), 129-131.

[4] James H. O'Donnell, Southern Indians in the American Revolution (Knoxville: University of Tennessee Press, 1973), 65-66.

[5] Caughey, McGillivray of the Creeks, 4.

subject to an habitual Head-Ach and Cholic".[6] McGillivray's own correspondences vividly reveal his chronically weak constitution. On one occasion, he noted that, "The Fever has reduced me very low & it has been succeeded by a breaking out over my body. I'm Apprehensive that I shall lose all my finger nails & tis with much difficulty, that I can take the pen in my hand to write."[7] The most detailed physical description of McGillivray describes him as possessing "a constitution by no means robust."[8] All of these physical accounts display an individual who was not suited for the physical rigors of eighteenth-century war.

Louis Milfort, one of McGillivray's war chiefs, confirmed his ailing health, but Milfort's written accounts detailing his time spent in the Creek Confederacy are questionable. Milfort himself returned to France after Alexander McGillivray's death. However, one must remember that Milfort's primary purpose for writing about his adventures within the Creek Confederacy was for political gain. Milfort had tried to persuade the French government to appoint him governor of the French territorial holdings of Louisiana. However, Napoleon Bonaparte's sale of this French territory (the Louisiana Purchase) to President Thomas Jefferson abruptly ended Milfort's bid for political power in North America.

Due to these facts, the French native's account of his activities and influence among the Creeks is, at times, bombastic and self-serving. Yet, even within Milfort's inflated prose, glimpses of historical truth are evident. Milfort openly mentions McGillivray's health issues, a detail that some historians have

---

[6] John Pope, A Tour Through The Southern and Western Territories of the United States of United States of North - America, (Richmond: John Dixion, 1792; reprint, Gainesville: University of Florida Press, 1979), 48.

[7] McGillivray to O'Neill, August 12, 1786, Caughey, McGillivray of the Creeks, 128.

[8] Albert J. Pickett, History of Alabama and Incidentally of Georgia and Mississippi From the Earliest Period vol. I (1851; reprint, Birmingham, Alabama: Birmingham Book and Magazine Co.,

interpreted as cowardice. For example, in one skirmish between McGillivray's Creek warriors and an American war party, Milfort notes that, "from the start of the battle, McGillivray hid in the bushes, were he remained until nightfall." He waited until the fighting was over and "then he left his hiding place and went courageously on the battlefield and stripped a dead Anglo-American of his clothes and covered himself with his cloak." McGillivray "was extremely cold" since he was naked and painted in Creek warrior fashion.[9]

Historians are fond of citing this account of McGillivray's actions during this battle, but their hasty judgment fails to notice other equally important descriptions of the Creek leader. Milfort believed that the "poor state of his [McGillivray's] health would make it impossible for him to endure the hardship[s] which accompany war; and that if he were forced to accept a position for which he was so badly fitted, the army would run the risk of being often without a chief, which could have grievous consequences."[10]

Alexander, clearly, did not fit the classic stereotype of a fierce Creek Indian or Scottish Highlander who were often depicted as possessing tremendous physical prowess. It is amazing that the Creek Confederacy, which often encouraged aggressive physical prowess among its warriors, accepted such a physically non-robust leader. McGillivray's ascendance as a leader debunks the historical stereotype of savage Indian tribes, led by an equally savage and physical war chief.

The Creek Confederacy's acceptance of Alexander McGillivray as a leader is a prime example of the Confederacy's forethought and shrewdness, as well as the influence of

---

1962), 345.

[9] Louis Milfort, Memoirs of a quick Glance at my various Travels and my Sojourn in the Creek Nation (Paris, 1802; reprint, Kennesaw, Georgia: Continental Book Company, 1959), 86.

[10] Ibid, 30.

McGillivray's well-placed kinship networks and diplomatic skills. These historical elements and attributes aided McGillivray in attaining acceptance as a Creek leader. The American Revolution marked a time in which the Creek Nation was experiencing increased pressure from the American colonies. Any individual who possessed solutions as to how the Creek Confederacy could maintain its political sovereignty would have been well received. Milfort surmised another reason for the Creek Indians' acceptance of Alexander, "When one has much administrative knowledge and as a noble heart as Alexander McGillivray had, one does not need military abilities to be a great man."[11]

.   .   .   .

In 1768 Sophia, a relative of Alexander, married David Taitt; a deputy to British Indian superintendents John Stuart and Thomas Brown. The exact relationship of Sophia to Alexander is still debated by scholars, with some historians claiming that it was Sehoy (II) McPherson who married David Taitt; but contemporary historians have argued that it was actually a Sophia McGillivray who married the British deputy. Sehoy (II) was Alexander McGillivray's step-sister whereas Sophia was his sister. Whichever case is the truth, the fact still remains that Alexander's family connections were beneficial in advancing his career. David Taitt's position as a British officer would have aided Alexander in his wartime assignment as an assistant commissary post.[12]

The exact date of McGillivray's appointment as a British officer is unknown, but his name first appeared in official British

---

[11] Milfort, Memoirs, 87.

[12] Thomas John Kennedy, "The Origins of Creek Indian Nationalism," (M. A. Thesis, University of Houston, 1992), 109-110; Edward J. Cashin, Lachlan McGillivray, Indian Trader: The Shaping of the Southern Colonial Frontier (Athens: University of Georgia Press, 1992), 73; For further discussion on Sehoy (II) see, Cashin, Lachlan McGillivray, 73-74, 333-334.

service documents on 21 September 1777.[13] The assignment of McGillivray to an assistant commissary position was a logical move for the British. Very few other individuals within the Creek Confederacy possessed access to the vast Scottish and Creek trade networks, but were still sternly anti-American/pro-British in their political convictions.[14]

Earlier historians stated that Alexander was commissioned as a colonel, but this claim is dubious and has been questioned by later historians. Some researchers question whether McGillivray ever became a full colonel because this rank was difficult to obtain during the eighteenth century, or at least when compared to later centuries.[15] Whether or not he served at the full rank of colonel is not important. The relevant point is McGillivray's comment in 1784 that, "I have Served his Brittanick Majesty for very near eight years past."[16] With a Loyalist (Pro-British) father and a mother from a large and prominent family, that was sympathetic to the British; Alexander's commission as a British officer was a natural conclusion. Knowledge of European culture and politics, as well as his prestigious Wind Clan connections, were helpful attributes for any Creek leader to possess.

.   .   .   .

By the beginning of hostilities that initiated the American Revolution, McGillivray had returned to his mother's tribal area in present day northern Alabama. McGillivray's loyalist (pro-British) convictions were intensified by the seizure of the McGillivray

[13] O'Donnell, "Alexander McGillivray," 173.

[14] William C. Sturtevant, "Commentary," In Eighteenth-Century Florida and Its Borderlands ed. Samuel Procter (Gainesville: The University Presses of Florida, 1975), 44.

[15] Albert Pickett in the 1850s was the first to publish that McGillivray was a British colonel; Pickett, History of Alabama II, 34. Caughey repeats this belief in 1938; Caughey, McGillivray of the Creeks, 16; James H. O'Donnell, "Alexander McGillivray," 174.

[16] McGillivray to O'Neill, January 3, 1784, (O'Neill was a Spanish official) Caughey, McGillivray of the Creeks, 66.

family's colonial property by American rebels. Lachlan was forced to give up substantial land holdings in and around both Savannah and Charleston.[17] Lachlan and Alexander's colonial property and possessions, which were confiscated by Georgian authorities, were valued at over $100,000.[18] Lachlan McGillivray fled to Scotland, taking with him what money and valuable objects he could collect on short notice. Lachlan's losses also affected Alexander who, through his father's will, was destined to possess a significant part of his father's property holdings. Alexander was to inherit a "garden lot of land west of the town of Savannah" as well as one-fifth of Lachlan's total colonial holdings. Tragically, however, Lachlan would outlive his son.[19] Not surprisingly, Alexander developed a significant anti-American sentiment due to his financial losses as well as the forced exodus of his father from the region.

Information concerning McGillivray's exact role in the American Revolution is vague due to the fact that many of his exact duties were not recorded. At the very least, his royal commission gave him direct entry into the ruling Creek Confederacy's government. As a British officer his primary task would have been to secure support for the British war effort within the Confederacy.[20] Other tasks likely included the organizing of Creek Indian war parties in order to attack neighboring rebel soldiers (usually Georgians).[21] However, this was not an easy task, even for one as politically connected as McGillivray. At the start of the

---

[17] Carolyn Thomas Foreman, "Alexander McGillivray, Emperor of the Creeks," Chronicles of Oklahoma 7 (March 1929): 109.

[18] William S. Coker and Thomas D. Watson, Indian Traders of the Southeastern Spanish Borderlands: Panton, Leslie & Company and John Forbes & Company, 1783-1847 (Pensacola: University of West Florida Press, 1986), 53.

[19] Lachlan McGillivray's will, June 12, 1767, State of Alabama Department of Archives and History, Montgomery, Alabama.

[20] Ibid, 16.

[21] Whitaker, "Alexander McGillivray, 1783-1789," 184.

American Revolution, the Creek Confederacy was split between pro-British and pro-American factions. McGillivray was never able to secure a fully unified pro-British Creek foreign policy, with the Confederacy officially maintaining a stance of neutrality during the Revolution.[22]

McGillivray's British commission provided him direct access to the Creek Confederacy's centralized government. His mother's influential Wind clan lineage meant that many of the Confederacy's council members were already responsive to the young leaders' ideas and suggestions. McGillivray's most immediate attribute was his fluency with the English language. One contemporary noted, "I spoke bad English to him which he understood immediately because he spoke that language perfectly".[23] The need for reliable, capable, and trustworthy interpreters was always a problem during the colonial period; with the Creek confederacy no exception to this fact. Any Confederacy member, who could communicate in English as well as any one of the myriad of Creek languages and dialects, would become a highly prized interpreter. In the end, McGillivray's British commission meant that he was politically positioned to assume the role of Creek-British interpreter for most of the Creek Confederacy.[24]

McGillivray's family kinship connections, combined with his educational experience, provided him an opportunity to transcend the role of a simple language interpreter. It must be remembered that the task of a good interpreter is to go beyond the literal translation from one language to another and understand the context. An interpreter who was thoroughly familiar with customs, traditions, as well as the language of both cultures; he

---

[22] Michael D. Green, "Alexander McGillivray," In R. David Edmunds ed. Studies in Diversity: American Indian Leaders (Lincoln and London: University of Nebraska Press, 1980), 45.
[23] Milfort, Memoirs, 19.
[24] Green, "Alexander McGillivray," 42-43.

likely not only translated the language, but also the foreign thoughts and motives behind the words.[25] By all historical accounts, McGillivray was an excellent interpreter. His possession of a classic eighteenth-century colonial education likely meant that he was able make English words and phrases become more than just "intelligible" to Creek Indian ears. His experience with European colonial society, along with this education, enabled the young American Indian leader to fully translate the wishes, policies, and cultural peculiarities of the Creek Confederacy's English-speaking neighbors. In this manner, McGillivray was aided by the fact that he, essentially, had been, "born with a foot in each culture."[26]

McGillivray's familiarity with Creek and Anglo-American cultures allowed the young assistant commissary to the British government to become more influential than his official title suggested. While working for the British, McGillivray's role as an interpreter began to become more dynamic and flexible. In addition to British and Creek diplomatic duties, he soon became an advisor to leaders of the Creek Indian Confederacy. Increasingly, leaders within the Confederacy valued his irreplaceable cultural insights and political advice.[27] The various pro-British connections that McGillivray had obtained during these years of service in the British Indian Department would prove useful in his future cultural-brokerage activities.[28] Coincidentally, whether by chance or design, Alexander's great-grandfather Farquhar had also been promoted to commissioner of supplies by the British Crown.

---

[25] Yasuhide Kawashima, "Forest Diplomats: The Role of Interpreters in Indian-White Relations on the Early American Frontier," Ethnohistory 13 (Winter 1989): 1.

[26] Nancy L. Hagedorn, "A Friend to Go Between Them': The Interpreter as Cultural Broker During Anglo-Iroquois Councils, 1740-70," Ethnohistory 35 (Winter, 1988): 62.

[27] Ibid, 8; Green, "Alexander McGillivray," 43.

[28] O'Donnell, "Alexander McGillivray," 182.

Alexander, like Farquhar, soon realized that individuals possessed a substantial amount of power when they controlled the supply of firearms, blankets, and food.

      •   •   •   •

The Creek Confederacy possessed a dualistic government structure that was split between civil councils and war councils. Civil councils consisted of tribal leaders (*micos*, *henihas*, and *beloved men*) who ruled the government and made policy decisions during times of peace. Eighteenth-century European travelers, who were accustomed to powerful monarchs, commented on the limited nature of the Creek civil branch of government; "The Powers of their Kings [council members] appear to be very circumscribed. . . being sometimes confined to a single Township, or a Spot of Ground not more than Ten Miles Square."[29]

During periods of warfare, Creek civil councils voluntarily relinquished their power to dominant tribal warriors who held positions within the war councils.[30] Once the period of conflict was over, the war councils would resign from power; allowing the civil councils to resume their traditional governing position. Curiously, after the American Revolution, the Creek war councils did not step down from political power. The civil councils were not allowed to resume their traditional political control.[31] The writings of the Frenchman Louis Milfort, McGillivray's brother-in-law who resided among the Creeks and became a military assistant, mentioned the

---

[29] Pope, A Tour, 65.

[30] John R. Swanton, Social Organization and Social Usage's of the Indians of the Creek Confederacy (Washington: United States Government Printing Office, 1924), 324-27; Edmunds, American Indian Leaders, 50.

[31] Swanton, Social Organization, 324-27; Green, "Alexander McGillivray," 50; Major Caleb Swan, Position and State of Manners and Arts in the Creek, or Muscogee Nation in 1791. Philadelphia, 1795; reprint in, Henry Rowe Schoolcraft, Historical and Statistical Information respecting the History, Conditions, and Prospects of the Indian Tribes of the United States 6 vols. (Philadelphia: Lippincott, Grambo, & Co, 1851-57), 5: 281.

dominance of military chiefs within Creek society. He noted that, "the Tastanagey or great war chief had, at first, no part in the domestic administration. His authority lasted only as long as the war; but, today, he is the head chief of the nation with respect to civil as well as military affairs."[32] This continuation of political control by the war councils would assist McGillivray in his rise to influence within the Creek Confederacy.

Contact with various European cultures caused many Native American societies to alter their political structure. Overall, European influences during the late sixteenth and seventeenth centuries transformed the southeastern region both demographically and technologically. Furthermore, diplomatic and economic pressures from the ever-encroaching European powers, forced tribal governments to become more centralized and vertically stratified.[33] Outside of the Creek Indians, the pressure to change long-established political structures in order to challenge European influences was also evident in other neighboring tribal societies. The Creek Confederacy's western neighbors and distant relatives, the Choctaws; were strongly influenced by French "pressures" filtering in from the Mississippi River valley and the Gulf of Mexico. As earlier as the 1740s, the Choctaws had stratified their political leadership into: tribal chief, district chiefs, war chiefs, village chiefs, and numerous assistants.[34]

The neighboring Cherokees to the North, traditionally sheltered by their homeland's mountainous topography,

---

[32] Milfort, Memoirs, 147.

[33] Patricia Galloway, "So Many Little Republics': British Negotiations with the Choctaw Confederacy, 1765," Ethnohistory 41 (Fall 1994): 514.

[34] Daniel H. Usner, Indians, Settlers, & Slaves in a Frontier Exchange Economy (Chapel Hill: University of North Carolina Press, 1992), 89; Further ethnographic information on the Choctaws in, John R. Swanton, Source Material for the Social and Ceremonial Life of the Choctaw Indians Bureau of American Ethnology Bulletin, no. 103, (Washington: United States Government Printing Office, 1931), 55-102.

experienced similar European pressures by the eighteenth century. Most of the Native American societies which had been located along the coast, near successful colonial settlements, had already been reduced by epidemics and wars into enclaves or refugee communities. Many Indian nations in the colonial hinterlands, in contrast, competed or negotiated successfully for economic advantages and political power. This was especially true with the fur trade networks that had expanded inland along major water routes. The Choctaws Nation firmly maintained a position of power in the Lower Mississippi Valley, resembling the Iroquois nations in New York and the Cherokees in Carolina.[35] The politically dominant Creek Confederacy of the southeastern pine woodlands was also struggling to negotiate and maintain economic and political influence within the region.

In McGillivray's lifetime, the political structure of the Creek Confederacy was a coalition of tribal fragments who were ambiguously committed to a general political alliance. However, the Confederacy's cultural diversity encouraged excessive local autonomy, with loyalties became increasingly weaker as one traveled beyond the boundaries of any specific village into the larger surrounding region of the Confederacy.[36] Repeated British attempts to consciously reform Creek political structures were always impeded by this deeply entrenched tradition of local autonomy. Often times, the British supported chiefs only sparingly, and grudgingly, knowing full well that the Indians would assume a "Creek" stance in their political outlook and overall interest.[37]

One must remember that the use of neutrality, as a political strategy, was an often used diplomatic tool by many of the

---

[35] Rennard Strickland, Fire and the Spirits: Cherokee Law from Clan to Court (Norman: University of Oklahoma Press, 1975), 40-53; Usner, Indians, Settlers, & Slaves, 77.

[36] Green, "Alexander McGillivray," 43.

[37] David H. Corkran, The Creek Frontier, 1540-1783, (Norman:

Native American societies within the region. Some historians have aptly pointed out that this practice of Creek Indian "low politics" in reality was simply a pragmatic "doctrine of neutrality."[38] American visitors noted in 1775 that, "the old men" of the Creek Confederacy were learning how to successfully respond to the growing influence of European colonialism. "Being long informed by the opposite parties, of the different views, and intrigues of those European powers, who paid them annual tribute under the vague appellation of presents, [they] were becoming surprisingly crafty in every turn of low politics. They held it as an invariable maxim, that their security and welfare required a perpetual friendly intercourse with us [the British] and the French."[39] In other words, the Creek Indians had learned how to force European powers to compete for the Confederacy's loyalty.

The Creek Indian policy of playing rival powers against each other, while remaining neutral, was a trait which McGillivray later redefined and developed to a new level. Usually, Native Americans supported whichever political power could supply the most trade goods, in both quality and quantity. McGillivray stated this fact clearly to the Spanish in his 1784 bid for protection when he noted that, "One Principal Consideration Should be a plentiful Supply of Goods . . . for the Indians will attach themselves to & Serve them best who Supply their Necessities."[40]

The inability to provide a steady supply of trade goods for Indian consumption was a major stumbling block for the American traders who were occupied with the American War for

University of Oklahoma Press, 1967), 249.

[38] Michael D. Green, The Politics of Indian Removal: Creek Government and Society in Crisis (Lincoln: University of Nebraska Press, 1982), 21; Corkran, The Creek Frontier, 1540-1783, 61.

[39] James Adair, History of the American Indians (London, 1775; reprint, New York: Argonaut Press, 1974), 277;

[40] McGillivray to O'Neill, January 1, 1784, Caughey, McGillivray of the Creeks, 65.

Independence.[41] A steady supply of rifles, powder, and rum were essential tools in maintaining a diplomatic balance within the Southeast. The Creek Indians' constant pursuit of valuable European manufactured products is readily demonstrated in the case of Spain's successful invasion of Mobile in March of 1780. Delegates from the Upper Creek tribes visited the new occupiers of the Mobile area, but did not enter into alliance with the Spanish. These negotiations were sabotaged due to the Creek's disappointment over the condition and quality of the Spanish gifts which had been presented to the neighboring Indian tribes.[42]

The ability for Creek leaders to maintain a balance between the various competing European rivalries was only possible through a constant supply of European manufactured firearms and ammunition.[43] The diplomatic connections that McGillivray had developed with the British government were based partially on the ability to consistently supply Creek Indians with English manufactured trade goods.[44] By the late-eighteenth century, any tribe which did not possess access to European weaponry was guaranteed to suffer a military defeat from the hands of their neighbors whether Indian, European, or American.[45]

The fragmented nature of Native American society troubled many of the European powers who sought to create diplomatic alliances. The political procedures of a tribal government did not always translate or correlate with the

---

[41] Corkran, The Creek Frontier, 1540-1783, 315.

[42] Ibid, 320.

[43] Caughey, McGillivray of the Creeks, 21.

[44] J. Leitch Wright Jr., Creeks & Seminoles: The Destruction and Regeneration of the Muscogulge People (Lincoln: University of Nebraska Press, 1986), 3; Verner W. Crane, "The Origins of the Name of the Creek Indians," Mississippi Valley Historical Review 5 (December 1918): 339-342.

[45] James Axtell, The Invasion Within: the Contest of Cultures in Colonial North America (Oxford: Oxford University Press, 1985), 289.

eighteenth-century European idea of a nation.[46] In their diplomatic relationships with the Creek Confederacy, the British adopted the practice of commissioning Creek war chiefs, who would act as British agents within their respected Creek towns.   European manufactured trade items, given as a gift or a bribe, were frequently used to cultivate relations with these war chiefs.[47] The main goal of these British military agents was to form a European-style chain of command, with tighten political control over the Creek government.[48]   However, in order for the British to accomplish this task; they would need educated individuals with strong Creek political connections who would openly oppose the Americans. A position that seemed made to order for Alexander.

     ·   ·   ·   ·

McGillivray's attainment of a British officer's position soon evolved into the role of organizing Creek war parties in order to support the British Crown during the Revolution. The full impact of his activities was only incidental to the overall outcome of the American Revolution. There were numerous Creek chiefs who took part in the War of Independence. However, the war did provide a means for McGillivray to display his leadership skills, as well as serves as an apprenticeship for future endeavors.[49]

Chance also played a role in McGillivray's ascent to a position of Creek political leadership. A smooth transition from an *interpreter* position to a *broker* position within the Confederacy would not have been possible without the death of Emistisiguo a

---

[46] For a deeper understanding of tribalism verses nationalism see, Morton H. Fried, The Notion of Tribe (Menlo Park, California: Cummings Publishing Company, 1975), 106-111.

[47] For further information on the ability of European powers to act like "patrons" over Indian "clients" refer to, chapter four, "Alexander McGillivray as a Leader: From 'Broker' to a 'Patron - Client' Relationship".

[48] Corkran, The Creek Frontier, 1540-1783, 27, 249.

[49] Caughey, McGillivray of the Creeks, 16; Whitaker, "Alexander McGillivray, 1783-1789," 184.

prominent Creek war chief. A *broker*, by definition, is an individual who is able to occupy an intermediate position between different groups.[50]   Emistisiguo was the head warrior of the Creek Confederacy and was pro-British in his sympathies. The death of the chief during a battle in June 1782 created a major political vacuum within the leadership of the anti-American Creek towns. McGillivray soon filled this vacuum, and by the summer of the following year, he had become one of the dominant Creek political leaders within the Confederacy.[51]   McGillivray's pro-British alliances, as well as range of influences and connections gained through years of service in the British Indian Department, provided a solid foundation for future cultural *brokerage* activities.[52]

.   .   .   .

American Indian societies had always tried to maintain a tolerable balance of power within the Southeast. However, European political and economic influences slowly transformed regional tribal governments. Due to European contact, and threats, the militaristic aspects of many Native American governments were forced to increase in power. Native American leaders with war or military connections soon dominated most Indian councils. The Native Americans of the region, and their practice of siding with European powers to maintain a regional diplomatic balance, soon developed into an anti-American ideology. Similarly, by the time of the American Revolution, Alexander McGillivray was thoroughly pro-Creek and pro-British in his cultural and political loyalties.

His father's British political orientation helped influence Alexander's sympathetic stance toward the English Crown. These pro-British loyalties combined with his influential family kinship

---

[50] Green, "Alexander McGillivray," 47.
[51] O'Donnell, Southern Indians in the American Revolution, 135; Corkran, The Creek Frontier, 249.
[52] O'Donnell, "Alexander McGillivray," 182.

connections and educational experiences; helped him to become a commissioned British officer during the American Revolution. This British commission further strengthened and expanded his political and economic connections and within the Creek Confederacy. With the passage of time, these cross-cultural connections and military alliances asserted an increasingly powerful influence on McGillivray's career.

Ultimately, Alexander's actions during the American Revolution demonstrated that he was a formidable and reliable Creek Indian war leader. During this same time period, due to McGillivray's rising influence; another European nation, with a vested interest in the Southeast, also noticed McGillivray's talents.

Chapter 3

♦

From Interpreter to Broker: 1784 - 1785

The outcome of the American Revolution, as well as the formalized border agreements from the 1783 Treaty of Paris, left the Creek Confederacy in a dire position. The land demands of the newly established United States of America, combined with the loss of British support, created problems on a catastrophic scale for many of the southeastern Indian tribes. The traditional sovereign and territorial holdings of the Creek Confederacy were under direct assault by the states of Georgia and South Carolina. By 1783, the Creek Indians were in a poor position to repel, or even challenge, the advance of American colonists upon Creek Confederacy lands.

The exodus of Loyalist backcountry traders, including McGillivray's Scottish father, Lachlan, severed some of the most crucial trade connections within the region. Without access to British merchandise, especially guns, shot, and powder; Creek Natives were unable to adequately defend their borders against armed Georgians and Carolinians. During this time, McGillivray increasingly used his influence as former interpreter, as well as family connections, to become one of the prevailing Creek leaders after the American Revolution. As a Native American leader, he was able to provide much needed European trade goods for the Creek Confederacy through his extensive trade connections.

Many of the backcountry trade networks were maintained even after the British government was officially expelled from the

Southeastern region following the American Revolution. These surviving trade linkages materialized with the founding of the Leslie & Panton Company; a trans-Atlantic Indian trading firm, which due to the influence of McGillivray, was allowed to operate out of Spanish controlled East Florida. This backcountry trade company relied heavily upon the trading of European goods within the Creek Confederacy, while simultaneously consolidated most of this trade. The development of a partnership between McGillivray and the Leslie & Panton Company, re-established a valuable trade connection for the Creek Confederacy. From the former role of *interpreter*, McGillivray quickly evolved into a *cultural broker*, and possessed considerable influence with the war chiefs who resided within the Confederacy's pro-military towns.

.　　　　　.　　　　　.　　　　　.

The Treaty of Paris officially ended the American Revolution on September 3, 1783. This treaty granted the United States its freedom from Great Britain, allowing the newly recognized states like Georgia to extend their western boundaries all the way to the Mississippi River. Before the war, both British and colonial governments had, at least to a degree, acknowledged that the indigenous tribes possessed the legal right of ownership to their land. This meant that the legal protocol of a formal treaty was required in order to purchase Native American owned territory. However, the colonial precedent of formal purchase was far from perfect. Numerous wars and injustices were committed against Native American populations by both European and American invaders. Nevertheless, the use of formal treaties, which at times were highly fraudulent, created a more orderly advance upon Native American land.[1]

---

[1] Reginald Horsman, "United States Indian Policies, 1776-1815," In Wilcomb Washburn <u>History of Indian-White Relations</u> vol. 4 William C. Sturtevant et al, ed. <u>Handbook of North American Indians</u> (Washington: Smithsonian Institution, 1988), 29;

The harsh years of fighting due to the American Revolution created, among many U. S. citizens, a bitter hatred of the Native Americans. This hatred was readily reflected in the Indian policy of the newly created United States of America. Much of this animosity was directed against Indian tribes who had actively supported the British Crown during the Revolutionary War. Congressional committee reports from the fall of 1783 and spring of 1784 brazenly placed Creek territory under American control.[2] The 1784 report fulfilled the Creek Confederacy's worst fears -- American citizens now believed that they were legally entitled to Creek Indian land. This belief was based on the principle that Native American tribes had forfeited their property rights when they had sided with the British during the American Revolution. Many Americans believed that the newly formed United States was justified in forcing the Creeks, and their tribal neighbors, to move west of the Mississippi River, an area already occupied by other Native American societies.[3]

However, there were additional reasons for the hostile stance that was clearly evident in America's early Native American foreign policy. The possibilities of obtaining wealth from the acquisition of this newly acquired land, as well as an inflated national confidence created by winning independence from one of the most powerful empires in the world, inspired the United States' initial Indian policy. The United States government assumed that

---

Yasuhide Kawashima, "Forest Diplomats: The Role of Interpreters in Indian-White Relations on the Early American Frontier" American Indian Quarterly 13 (Winter, 1989): 8; Francis Jennings, The Invasion of America: Indians, Colonialism, and the Cant of Conquest (Chapel Hill: University of North Carolina Press, 1975), 124; Francis Jennings, The Ambiguous Iroquois Empire: The Covenant Chain Confederation of Indian Tribes with English Colonies from Its Beginning to the Lancaster Treaty of 1744 (New York: W. W. Norton & Company, 1984), 63.

[2] Worthington C. Ford, et al, ed., Journals of the Continental Congress, 1774-1789, 34 vols. (Washington: United States Government Printing Office, 1904-1937), vol. 25: 681-693, vol. 27: 453-465.

[3] William C. Sturtevant, et al, ed., Handbook of North American

most Native American societies, shocked by the defeat of their British ally, would willingly surrender their land. This was believed even though many Indian tribes were militarily never defeated during the Revolutionary War.

The Americans demanded Indian land cessions as reparation for hostilities during the war. Some U. S. government officials had hoped to establish boundary lines that would allow Indian tribes to possess land within the borders of the United States. If the right of territorial sovereignty belonged to the United States, Native Americans could then only remain within this occupied territory by permission from the U. S. Federal government. Ultimately, the primary goal of United States' relations with the American Indians, following the 1783 Treaty of Paris, was to acquire land; peace existed only as a secondary goal.[4]

A major problem for the Creek Confederacy arose due to the ever-expanding land demands of Georgian settlers. Because of these territorial issues, Creek Confederacy relations with the United States government and the separate states, was marked by a longer history of conflict than those of any other major southern Indian tribe. As previous scholars have pointed out, the Creek Confederacy was an "amalgam of the dominant Muskogee group with smaller tribes displaced by advancing pioneers, . . . resisting white encroachment . . . by warfare." In other words, the only reason that the Creeks existed, was as a defensive response to earlier "waves" of invading European diseases and peoples.[5]

Creek linguistic terms for describing the Georgians demonstrated the Native American's concern over American expansion. By the eighteenth century, the Creeks had developed a

---

Indians, 29.

[4] Ibid, 29-30.

[5] Mary Elizabeth Young, Redskins, Ruffleshirts and Rednecks: Indian Allotments in Alabama and Mississippi, 1830-1860 (Norman: University of Oklahoma Press, 1961), 35.

unique descriptive term for their Georgian neighbors: "E·cun·naw·nux·ulga," which meant "people greedily grasping after the lands of the red man."[6] This term was close to the truth, due to the fact that the population of Georgia was expanding. Population pressures, as well as the lure of cheap and fertile land, were the key motivating factors behind the pursuit of Creek Indian territory. Most of Georgia's population increases occurred during the decades prior to the American Revolution. In 1773 alone, the Creek Confederacy had surrendered 2,100,000 acres of its territory to the Georgian government. However, by the close of the American Revolution in 1783, there were increasingly vocal and aggressive demands for additional western land.[7]

Georgia, like most other newly formed U. S. states, saw western lands as an excellent way to raise revenue for its nearly bankrupt state treasury. The state of Georgia was fairly poor in regards to available financial resources, yet land was the one commodity it considered an asset. The newly formed United States, also nearly bankrupt, possessed a major stake in the pursuit of Indian controlled territory to the West. A sizable amount of politicians felt that this territorial area rightly belonged to the fledging republic because of its victory over Great Britain.[8]

Britain's defeat at the hands of the Americans was a shock for McGillivray, as well as many other American Indian tribes who had traded with the English for many decades. Shock quickly turned to insult as the British left the Indians, who had actively supported the Crown, to fend for themselves against the invading

---

[6] James E. Calloway, The Early Settlement of Georgia (Athens: University of Georgia Press, 1948), vii.

[7] Louis DeVorsey, "Indian Boundaries in Colonial Georgia," Georgia Historical Quarterly 54 (Spring, 1970): 72-75.

[8] Mary Ann Oglesby Neeley, "Alexander McGillivray, Diplomatic Leader of the Creeks: 1783-1793," (M.A. Thes., Auburn University, 1973), 54.

American settlers.[9] A prominent Creek Confederacy Indian named
Fine Bones, epitomized the dominant Creek sentiment in a speech
delivered in St. Augustine on May 1, 1783:

> *The old beloved men informed me that the warriors of my*
> *town first joined the English as men and friends -- that*
> *they gave them lands and became one flesh -- that they*
> *considered their enemies as our own -- that in all the wars*
> *either against Indians, Spaniards, or Virginians, they*
> *assisted them -- that they often took prisoners whom the*
> *English redeemed and had children by them who live*
> *among us -- Do the English mean to abandon their own*
> *children with their friends? Why will they turn their backs*
> *on us and forsake us? We never expected that men and*
> *warriors our friends would throw us into the hands of our*
> *enemies.*[10]

Statements made by Commandant McArthur of the St.
Augustine garrison reinforced Fine Bones' words: "The minds of
these people [the Creeks] appear as much agitated as those of the
unhappy Loyalists . . . having made all the world their enemies by
their attachment to us."[11]

McGillivray's feelings of shock and betrayal were expressed
in a letter to the British government which possessed many of the
same sentiments as the speech made by Fine Bones:

---

[9] James H. O'Donnell, <u>Southern Indians in the American Revolution</u>
(Knoxville: University of Tennessee Press, 1973), 130.

[10] Talk of *Fine Bones* of Coweta, May 15, 1783, British Public
Record Office -- Colonial Office Group, Class 5, Piece 82, pp.
746-47.

[11] *McArthur to Carleton*, May 19, 1783, James H. O'Donnell,
<u>Southern Indians in the American Revolution</u>. 131.

[It was] not from a sense of Particular Injury Received by us from these people [the Americans] that we waged war but from principles of Gratitude and Friendship to the British Nation whose repeated Calls for assistance we cheerfully obeyed and after a nine years contest during which this Nation [the Creek] gave proof of unshaken fidelity and at the close of it to find ourselves and country betrayed to our Enemies and divided between the Spanish and Americans is Cruel and ungenerous.[12]

.   .   .   .

While an American victory brought a sense of betrayal for the Creeks, it also meant the forced exodus of English and Scottish merchants who had remained loyal to the British government. The absence of Indian traders, such as Lachlan McGillivray, disrupted many of the long-established Creek trade networks. The expulsion of merchants also created a critical shortage of European trade goods within the Confederacy. Without a steady supply of European products, especially rifles, powder, and shot; the Creeks would fall prey to the more heavily armed Americans. However, McGillivray solved the Confederacy's supply problem by establishing new trade connections with the Spanish government in the territories of East and West Florida. His trade links with the Spanish ultimately propelled McGillivray from the position of an *interpreter* to a more influential *brokerage* relationship between the Creek Confederacy and the Spanish Crown.

Fate played a role in McGillivray's ascent to a position of leadership within the Creek Confederacy. A smooth transition from an *interpreter* to a *broker* position would not have been possible without the death of Emistisiguo a prominent Creek war chief.

---

[12] *McGillivray* to *Brown*, August 30, 1783, British Public Record

Emistisiguo was the "principal warrior of the Creek Nations," who was pro-British in his sympathies.[13] The death of the chief during a battle in June 1782, created a major political vacuum in the leadership of the anti-American Creek towns. By the summer of following year, Alexander McGillivray had become a dominant Creek Indian leader within the Confederacy.[14] McGillivray's pro-British connections as well as range of influences, partially developed through years of service in the British Indian Department, would further his cultural brokerage activities.[15]

The years 1783 and 1784 marked a critical turning point in both the evolution of McGillivray's career and the overall political dynamic of the Southeast. This period was important for McGillivray due to the fact that he would enter into negotiations with Spain, which eventually led to the Treaty of Pensacola on June 1, 1784. This treaty was a pragmatic act of diplomacy and an expected action for the devoutly anti-American McGillivray. However, to fully understand the motivations behind the Treaty of Pensacola, details from the years immediately before its signing require discussion.

The Spanish capture of Pensacola in 1781 had severed the most direct line of trade between the British and many of the Creek Confederacy's towns. During the American Revolution, the evacuation of British troops from Savannah and Charleston in 1782 had worsened trade conditions, leaving only East Florida under British control in the southern theater. In addition, the British realized that the trade-starved Creek Indians would become a

---

Office -- Colonial Office Group, Class 5, Piece 82, 811-12.

[13] *Wayne* to *Greene*, June 24, 1782, Papers of the Continental Congress, no. 155, II, 492.

[14] James H. O'Donnell, Southern Indians in the American Revolution, 135; David H. Corkran, The Creek Frontier, 1540-1783 (Norman: University of Oklahoma Press, 1967), 249.

[15] James H. O'Donnell, "Alexander McGillivray: Training for Leadership, 1777-1783," Georgia Historical Quarterly 49 (June, 1965): 182.

problem if trade obligations were not met. The demand for trade goods would force the Creeks to open trade relations with any party that could successfully supply them with trade goods. In order to prevent this occurrence, British officials endorsed the establishment of a loyalist Indian trading company in East Florida which went by the named Panton, Leslie, and Company.[16]

The original founding partners of the Panton, Leslie, and Company were William Panton, John Leslie, Thomas Forbes, Charles McLatchy, and William Alexander.[17] In regards to the career of Alexander McGillivray, Panton was the most influential and important. Alexander, years earlier, had likely first met Panton in the colonial harbor towns of Charleston or Savannah during the late 1760s or early 1770s. It is also highly probable that William Panton's business dealings during the decades immediately before the American Revolution would have brought him into contact with Lachlan McGillivray. One must remember that both McGillivray and Panton were of Scottish ancestry. The connections between the McGillivrays and Panton's trading company were most likely a natural extension of the earlier, pre-revolution, Scottish dominated trade networks.[18]

William Panton founded the Panton, Leslie, and Company in East Florida in late 1782 or early 1783, with the company established before the British owners were even aware that East Florida was destined to become part of the Spanish Empire. When

---

[16] Thomas D. Watson, "Strivings For Sovereignty: Alexander McGillivray, Creek Warfare, and Diplomacy, 1783-1790," Florida Historical Quarterly 58 (April, 1980): 402; Thomas D. Watson, "The Troubled Advance of Panton, Leslie and Company into Spanish West," Eighteenth Century Florida and the Revolutionary South, Samuel Proctor ed., (Gainesville: The University Presses of Florida, 1978), 68.

[17] William S. Coker and Thomas D. Watson, Indian Traders of the Southeastern Spanish Borderlands: Panton, Leslie & Company and John Forbes & Company, 1783-1847 (Pensacola: University of West Florida Press, 1986), 15-30.

[18] Ibid, 24; Carolyn Thomas Foreman, "Alexander McGillivray, Emperor of the Creeks," Chronicles of Oklahoma 7 (March, 1929):

the end of British rule in East Florida occurred in 1784, three out of the five partners -- McLatchy, Leslie, and Panton -- remained in the Floridas.[19] But why would a pro-British trading firm, owned by English and Scottish loyalist, be allowed to remain in Spanish occupied territory?

The answer is the influence of Alexander McGillivray who already possessed a close connection to Panton's and trading company. When it became evident that the British planned to evacuate St. Augustine, the last remaining source of English goods for the Creek Indians; McGillivray approached Panton and urged him stay and maintain the Indian trade. McGillivray convinced Panton to maintain his trading stores in Florida by late 1783 or early 1784. Panton agreed to stay and maintain his trading company, only if McGillivray agreed to become a business partner and guarantee the overall safety of Panton's Indian trading operation. Panton's request that McGillivray assume a partnership in the trading company became a reality with the signing of the Treaty of Pensacola in June 1784.[20]

Spanish officials feared that the shortage of European trade goods among the various southeastern Indian tribes would force Native Americans to seek trade alliances with the United States. In 1783, the Spanish official Arturo O'Neill noted that "it seems to me advisable to keep the friendship of Maguilberi [McGillivray] and other Creoles living in the nations and of such Englishman. . . , since in what other fashion can we be assured of the trade and friendship of the Indians, who at present are strongly opposed to the name of Americans."[21] The former British posts on

109.
[19] William S. Coker and Thomas D. Watson, Indian Traders, 42-43.
[20] Ibid, 24; Jerrel Shofner, Florida Portrait: A Pictorial History of Florida (Sarasota, Florida: Pineapple Press Inc., 1990), 50.
[21] O'Neill to Ezpeleta, October 19, 1783, John Walton Caughey, McGillivray of the Creeks (Norman: University of Oklahoma Press,

the St. Johns River in East Florida were the only remaining trade outlets in the region, and they were far too remote to serve the supply demands of the entire southeastern region.   However, Spanish officials saw the benefit of working with an experienced Indian trade company which already possessed well-established economic connections.   If Spain was to capitalize upon its repossession of the Floridas from Great Britain, then trade with the Creek Confederacy had to be reinstated as quickly as possible. Spanish officials realized that since the Creek Confederacy had maintained a pro-British stance during the American Revolution, after the war many Creeks possessed anti-American sentiments.[22]

Anti-American feelings within the Creek Confederacy were intensified by the 1783 Treaty of Augusta.   This treaty clearly indicated that the former colony of Georgia was setting out on a policy of western expansion.   In the previous decades, Georgia's desire to expand westward had been held in check by the British government.   For Georgia, the treaty was the start of an unrestrained era of aggressive territorial expansion at the expense of Native American tribes.   Georgia claimed an exclusive right to enact a treaty with the Creek Indians, who in November of 1783, were forced to relinquish a significant amount of the Confederacy's territory to the Georgians.   As compensation for damages received during the American Revolution from pro-British Creek raids, the treaty transferred to Georgia over 800 square miles of land along the eastern border of the Creek Confederacy.[23]

Financial concerns were also a critical motivating factor behind Georgia's pursuit of the Treaty of Augusta.   The newly

1938),   62;   Lucille Griffith,   Alabama: A Documentary History to 1900   (Alabama: University of Alabama Press,   1968),   44.
[22] Lucille Griffith,   Alabama: A Documentary History to 1900,   13-14,   44.
[23] Michael D. Green,   "Alexander McGillivray,"   In   Studies in Diversity: American Indian Leaders,   ed.   R. David Edmunds (Lincoln and London: University of Nebraska Press,   1980),   46;

recognized state's desire to re-open trade linkages with the Native American population, as well as regain lost financial assets, was clearly expressed in the first two articles of the 1783 treaty. The first article states: "That all differences between the said parties heretofore subsisting shall cease and be forgotten." While the second article states: "That all just debts due by any of the said Indians to any of the merchants or traders of the said state, shall be fairly and fully paid; and all negroes, horses, cattle or other property taken during the late war, shall be restored."[24]

Soon after the ending of the American Revolution in 1783, Americans quickly began to pressure the Creek Confederacy for land. This pursuit of Native American land had started long before the American Revolution, but the removal of Great Britain from the southeastern region triggered an even greater land hunger among the citizens of the newly formed United States of America. Under these circumstances McGillivray led a group of Creek leaders to speak with the new Spanish governor of Pensacola, Arturo O' Neill.[25] The corresponding treaty that was generated from this meeting with the Spanish was the Treaty of Pensacola.[26]

.   .   .   .

The signing of the Treaty of Pensacola on June 1, 1784 was McGillivray's first major public act performed on behalf of the Creek Confederacy. In the negotiations leading up to the treaty, a central tenet of McGillivray's foreign policy is clearly evident. He believed the Creek Confederacy was a free and sovereign nation, whose inhabitants possessed the right of self-determination.[27] In

William S. Coker and Thomas D. Watson, Indian Traders, 55.

[24] Treaty of Augusta, November 1, 1783, in Linda Grant DePauw, ed., Senate Executive Journal and Related Documents (Baltimore and London: Johns Hopkins University Press, 1974), 2:166.

[25] William S. Coker and Thomas D. Watson, Indian Traders, 55.

[26] Mary Ann Oglesby Neeley, "Alexander McGillivray, Diplomatic Leader of the Creeks: 1783-1793" (M. A. Thes., Auburn University, 1973), 34, 44.

[27] Michael D. Green, "Alexander McGillivray," In Studies in

McGillivray's description of his appeal for help from the Spanish governor at Pensacola, the young leader noted that he had:

> *offer'd to put the Creek Nation under his Most Catholic Majestys Protection, as the americans pretend that we are in their Boundary. If the British Nation has been Compell'd to Withdraw its protection from us, She has no right to give up a Country she never could call her own. Therefore as a free Nation we have an undoubted right to choose what Protection we think proper.*[28]

He was also motivated by a concern to "be rendered & Kept Independent of the American States." The Creek Indian leader proposed an alliance with Spain, "So that we Shall be enabled to Continue our resistance with effect & to preserve our Lands, any cessions of Which we are determined never to Consent to."[29]

The Treaty of Pensacola was advantageous for both the Creek Confederacy and the Spanish controlled territories of East and West Florida. In the first article of the treaty the Confederacy agreed, "to Keep and Maintain an Inviolable Peace and fidelity, with his Most Catholick Majesty his provinces, Subjects, and vassals."[30] However, the Treaty of Pensacola did not guarantee the Creek Confederacy's right for territorial sovereignty. The treaty merely agreed to protect any Creek territory which fell within the limits of Spanish boundaries. Alexander was awarded with an appointment as the Confederacy's Spanish commissary, receiving a

---

Diversity: American Indian Leaders, ed. R. David Edmunds, 48.

[28] *McGillivray* to *Miro*, March 28, 1784, John Walton Caughey, McGillivray of the Creeks, 73.

[29] McGillivray to intendant-General Martin Navarro, November 7, 1785, D.C. Corbitt ed. tr., "Papers Relating to the Georgia-Florida Frontier, 1784-1800," Georgia Historical Quarterly 21 (March, 1937): 75.

[30] John Walton Caughey, McGillivray of the Creeks, 75; *Miro* to *McGillivray*, June 7, 1784, Ibid, 77; Ibid, 25.

salary of fifty dollars a month. McGillivray's diplomatic pursuits were crucial for providing stability to the region while simultaneously encouraging trade. This fact is illustrated by the treaty's third article which stated, "In order more and more to encourage the Commerce, and agriculture, the Creek Nations will establish a General Peace with the Chickasaws, Chactaws, and other nations of the Continent."[31]

Amazingly, with the ratification of the Treaty of Pensacola, military and economic interest, which were initially unconnected, came under control of the Panton, Leslie & Company. This British trading company's reach would extend throughout the Creek Confederacy as well as into the Chickasaws and Choctaws territory. This commerce originated out of a Spanish controlled territory, and only operated with the King of Spain's good graces. Out of all these various interests, Alexander McGillivray was at the center, with these separate economic, political, and cultural "lines" all converging to his position.

In hindsight, it becomes clear as to why McGillivray, during the 1784 treaty negotiations, tried to convince the Spanish to extend the Panton, Leslie & Company's trading territory to Pensacola and Mobile. McGillivray was denied this request and Panton was granted the right only to conduct business out of his trading post near St. Augustine. The reason that McGillivray's trading company was denied access to Western Florida was because the Spanish governors had made prior commitments. A trading firm out of New Orleans, by the name Mather and Strother, had already been granted the privilege of conducting trade in the area from Mobile to Pensacola. If McGillivray's request had been granted, the Indian trading company that he was associated with

---

[31] Ibid, 76.

would have gained a monopoly over the entire region's trade network.[32]

The complexity of Alexander McGillivray's diplomatic maneuvering, and the full extent of the negotiations which took place in mid-1784, are far more intricate than they first appear. For example, McGillivray trading partner William Panton, who was not present at the signing of the Treaty of Pensacola, was unaware of the fact that a business rival had also attended the signing of the treaty. James Mather of the New Orleans-based firm of Mather and Strother, who possessed the support of the Spanish governors, had attempted to solicit McGillivray's friendship. When McGillivray mentioned his connection with Panton's trading firm, a Spanish officer advised the Creek Indian leader against flatly refusing Mather's offer. This warning was based on the fact that Mather's trading firm possessed significant influence on the area and, "he could prejudice any other trading business" and its dealings with the Spanish.[33]

McGillivray did not immediately accept Mather's business proposal, but by December 1784 the Creek Indian leader agreed to become involved with Mather's New Orleans based business. The Mather and Strother firm traditionally had only conducted trade relations with the Choctaws and Chickasaws, but they were quite willing to expand their base of operations further east in order to include the Creek Confederacy. Even though McGillivray keep his connection to Mather's business a secret, he still favored Panton's trading firm; and pressed heavily for the Scottish company to become the dominant trade force in the Pensacola region.[34]

---

[32] Ibid, 24-25.

[33] *McGillivray* to *McLatchy*, October 4, 1784, Ibid, 82-83; William S. Coker and Thomas D. Watson, Indian Traders, 61.

[34] *McGillivray* to *McLatchy*, December 25, 1784, John Walton Caughey, McGillivray of the Creeks, 84-87; William S. Coker and Thomas D. Watson, Indian Traders, 61.

McGillivray's correspondence to the Spanish, for almost two years following the Treaty of Pensacola, contained numerous favorable references in regards to Panton's company. He argued to Spanish authorities that goods shipped by Mather and Strother were insufficient, or were only shipped on an irregular basis. With the major premise of his argument resting on the uncertainty of the Mather and Strother trade, McGillivray presented Panton, Leslie & Company as a necessary replacement. In fact, McGillivray had told the truth when he advocated Panton, Leslie & Company as a viable alternative to Mather and Strother.[35]

The Mather and Strother Company had experienced difficulties in conducting the backcountry trade in West Florida. Permission had been granted to the firm by the controlling Spanish government to import two shiploads of English goods, one to Mobile and the other to Pensacola. However, the firm's credit had only allowed for one shipload of goods, which would have left Pensacola without any European trade merchandise. William Panton's company volunteered to fill the supply shortage by exporting goods from St. Augustine and the Bahamas. In this fashion the Panton, Leslie & Company was able to gain access to the Pensacola trade network. Initially, the company was issued a series of temporary trade permits by the Spanish authorities, which eventually expanded into a total monopolization of the southeastern Indian trade and most of its domestic commerce.[36] McGillivray's letters to the Spanish officials explicitly state that, "Mr. Panton who has been long connected in this business & well Inclined to forward the Views of Government within his line. . . is most Capable & able to furnish Goods equal to the Demand of the Indians".[37]

---

[35] John Walton Caughey, <u>McGillivray of the Creeks</u>, 25-26.
[36] Ibid, 25-26.
[37]*McGillivray to O'Niell*, July 24, 1785 Ibid, 94.

McGillivray was doing what most Native American leaders were trying to do during the tumultuous disruptions of the eighteenth century -- maintain their people's political and territorial sovereignty. Originally, the fact that one trading company would control the entire supply of European goods worried the Creek leader. The Confederacy had recently experienced the negative consequences of adhering to a single supply source policy with the defeat of the British during the American Revolution. The Creek Confederacy desperately needed trade goods and Alexander was ensuring that his people, and nation, never found itself in this predicament again; while coincidently making a respectable profit.

The Treaty of Pensacola provided the Creek Confederacy with a guaranteed supply of European trade goods, as well as a pledge of support for the protection of their territory within Spanish controlled Florida. It authorized the development of trade, which was soon fully controlled by the Loyalist refugee firm Panton, Leslie & Company, with McGillivray possessing a silent partnership in the firm. McGillivray's diplomatic skills provided the Creek Confederacy access to Spanish aid which included a pledge from Spain that large amounts of guns and powder would be available for the defense of the Creek Indians' borders.[38] The Confederacy's ability to have regular access to European ammunition became a key element in their ability to resist invading American settlers. With the Treaty of Pensacola, McGillivray had simultaneously solved two of the critical issues facing the Creek Indians following the Revolution: territorial acknowledgment and access to European trade goods.

       •   •   •   •

---

[38] Michael D. Green, "Alexander McGillivray," In Studies in Diversity: American Indian Leaders, ed. R. David Edmunds, 48; Jack Holmes, "Spanish Treaties with West Florida Indians, 1784-1802," Florida Historical Quarterly 68 (October 1969): 140-145.

The Treaty of Pensacola marked another major step in McGillivray's career. The former British officer and interpreter was now, not only a prominent Indian leader; but also a Spanish Commissary for the Creek Confederacy. Earlier Scottish/Creek trade networks, which were established and maintained through Lachlan McGillivray and Sehoy's influence, eventually allowed Alexander to create a business alliance with the Panton, Leslie & Company and a secret partnership with the Spanish backed trading firm of Mather and Strother.

Ultimately, this international linkage with Spain gave McGillivray greater political and diplomatic dominance in southeastern region. These diplomatic maneuverings provided him with greater individual control of trade, which in turn increased his ability to influence and shape the region's political decisions. In many societies, the individuals who controlled the region's trade routes were often able to gain a greater degree of the area's political influence. For example, similar events took place among many of the northeastern Indian tribes who were caught between French, English, and American interest. Among the Huron tribes of the northeast, the control of trade goods and trade routes provided an important method for acquiring wealth and influence.[39]

McGillivray had evolved from a simple interpreter into a *broker* or *mediator* for the Creek Confederacy. The concept of a cultural broker in this historical context is aptly summarized "as simultaneous members of two or more interacting networks (kin groups, political factions, communities, or other formal or informal coalitions) a broker provides nodes of communication; with respect to a community's relations with the outside world, they stand guard over the crucial junctures or synapses of relationships which

---

[39] Brian M. Fagan, Clash of Cultures (New York: W. H. Freeman and Company, 1984), 196.

connect the local system to the larger whole."[40] Other historians have defined the McGillivray of the early 1780s as a "power broker between the Spanish and Americans."[41]

A more complete definition of a cultural broker refers to an individual who is able to occupy an intermediate position between different groups, societies, or cultures. This position is usually one step removed from the final responsibility of decision making, which sometimes allows a broker to promise more than he or she can deliver.[42] The talented use of diplomatic skills allows these individuals to promote the goals of one party while protecting the interest of another, which ultimately becomes crucial to all involved groups.[43] This description of a cultural broker fully encompasses McGillivray's economic and political activities by 1784, yet this definition fails to fully explain the complexity of the Creek leader's political, economic, and cultural connections.

The conventional definition of a "broker" portrays a person who wields power from a very fragile, almost non-existent base. The broker's power depends upon the extent to which he or she is able to deceive each party. A true broker, by the narrowest sense of the word, is sometimes forced to bluff his or her way through negotiations with outside parties. They provide a critical tie-in or *nexus* between two previously unrelated groups, creating a base of workable influence from this arrangement. McGillivray, by the treaty of Pensacola in 1784, had started to expand beyond the strict definition of cultural broker.

---

[40] Daniel K. Richter, "Cultural Brokers and Intercultural Politics: New York-Iroquois Relations, 1664-1701," Journal of American History 75 (June, 1988): 41.

[41] Michael D. Green, "Alexander McGillivray," In Studies in Diversity: American Indian Leaders, ed. R. David Edmunds, 47.

[42] Margaret Connell Szasz ed., Between Indian and White Worlds. (Norman: University of Oklahoma Press, 1994), 11.

[43] Daniel K. Richter, "Cultural Brokers and Intercultural Politics: New York-Iroquois Relations, 1664-1701," 41;

During the American Revolution McGillivray had expanded his personal political connections and experiences. His start as an interpreter for the British Royal Crown among the Creek Indians became a jumping point for him to transition into more complex cultural "brokerage" activities. These actions soon materialized with his ascendancy after the Revolution as an important Creek leader, initially based on his family's heritage as well as his ability to communicate and work with competing political entities. The connections that McGillivray established between the Creek Confederacy, the Spanish government, and a Scot-dominated Loyalist trading company created a substantial culture brokerage position. This consolidation of power by Alexander McGillivray not only connected "lines" of political communication and economic exchange in the Southeast, but eventually began to control the political events within the region.

The 1783 Treaty of Paris removed the military presence of Great Britain in the southeastern backcountry and officially recognized the independence of the United States of America. However, this treaty also placed the entire Creek Confederacy in a position of jeopardy. The loss of British military and economic support and the aggressiveness of the newly formed American nation, lead to a direct invasion of the Confederacy's traditional borders. The lack of European goods within the Confederacy, specifically rifles and ammunition, meant that the Creek Indians would have a difficult time trying to repel the territorial advances of the Americans. McGillivray's access to established trade networks, cross-cultural knowledge, and diplomatic abilities provided the Creeks with access to European trade goods; as well as an alliance with a European nation that could counter the territorial advances of the Americans.

McGillivray's direct business relationship with the Leslie, Panton & Company allowed him to strength his influence throughout the Creek Confederacy, especially in the Upper Creek war towns which were primarily controlled by members of his mother's family, the Wind clan. The Leslie, Panton & Company funneled Spanish and English goods into the Creek Confederacy. This ability to supply valuable trade goods after the American Revolution, as well as some diplomatic protection from the Americans; placed McGillivray in a position of leadership within the Confederacy. Even though McGillivray was not officially a chief, by 1784 the young Creek leader and former British officer had moved from the role of an interpreter to the more influential and complex role of a cultural broker.

Chapter 4

♦

From Broker to Patron - Client: 1785 - 1790

The Panton, Leslie, and Company conducted trade in the Creek Confederacy only with the blessing of Alexander McGillivray. This act alone placed the Native American leader in a favorable political and economic position. The trading company was only allowed to conduct business out of trading post in Spanish-controlled Florida due to the diplomatic maneuvering of McGillivray. The young Creek leader depended on Spain for military protection, while the Panton, Leslie, and Company was forced to rely on the good graces of the McGillivray and his ability to maintain beneficial relationship with the Spanish Crown. McGillivray was rapidly moving from a broadly defined *brokerage* position of power into a Patron-Client relationship with Spain. However, this Patron-Client relationship was soon tested when the state of Georgia invaded the Creek Confederacy's eastern borders.

In the 1780s, the Creek Indians conducted a successful defense of their borders against Georgian incursions, a success that was aided by the contribution of Spanish weapons and ammunition. The bargaining power that McGillivray possessed through his control of the Confederacy's trade connections and routes displays an increasingly dynamic political power base. This new found influence actually allowed him to create unique political structures within the Confederacy. McGillivray's attempted to reorganize the Confederacy's government in order to fit a more broadly defined concept of a "Creek" Nation. The Native American leader displayed a style of leadership which blended economic, political, and military traditions under his centralized authority.

However, the changes that McGillivray introduced were not always easily implemented. Both the neighboring Georgians and McGillivray used direct, and sometimes violent, methods to achieve their individual goals. Different traditions and interpretations of governmental power and authority within the Confederacy itself, created a baffling array of problems for the Creek leader. The political complexity of the southeastern region, as well as the overall Creek Confederacy; limited some of the possibilities available to any leader. Nevertheless, McGillivray's cultural fluidity and diplomatic shrewdness fueled his success and allowed him to consolidate power.

·   ·   ·   ·

McGillivray's Scottish trade connections with William Panton created a considerable base of influence within the Southeast, or what the newly founded United States referred to as "the southwestern frontier".[1] Pre-American Revolution Scottish trading connections provided a crucial reference point for McGillivray, which in later years were expanded. The establishment of Panton, Leslie & Company was greatly aided by McGillivray's relationship with the Spanish government. The granting of Spanish protection allowed the Scottish trading firm, as well as McGillivray, to possess a monopoly over most of the southeastern regions backcountry trade; which was sanctioned and protected by the Spanish governors in both East and West Florida.

---

[1] *George Washington* to the *U. S. Senate*, August 11, 1790, John C. Fitzpatrick ed., The Writings of George Washington: from Original Manuscript Sources, 1745-1799 (Washington: United States Government Printing Office, 1939), 88; J. Leitch Wright, "Creek-American Treaty of 1790: Alexander McGillivray and The Diplomacy of the Old Southwest," Georgia Historical Quarterly 21 (December, 1967): 379; Florette Henri, The Southern Indians and

Due to this fact, within a few years Panton, Leslie, and Company had absorbed most of the region's Indian trade. The astute Scottish business partners made the most of this opportunity, which was only made possible because of the political maneuverings of McGillivray.[2]

Alexander McGillivray was rapidly becoming the dominant figure in the overall Southeastern backcountry, due to his connections to both Panton and the Spanish government. However, McGillivray was heavily dependent upon the trading company's ability to provide a seemingly never-ending line of credit. Not surprisingly, when McGillivray died, he was heavily in debt to the trading company. The Creek leader's personal letters portray the uneasiness he felt about his financial dependence on Panton's trading company:

> *Here am I an Absolute heavy Tax upon you for several years, and in fact not only for my private Support, but for all extra Expenses of this department, and although my dear sir I know that I can Still depend upon your generosity and in your friendship that you overlook the heavy Expense I put you to, yet you well know how hurtful it is to the feeling heart to be beholden to Subsist wholly on the bounty of private friendship.*[3]

McGillivray's debt to Panton is further demonstrated in a death notice sent by the Scottish merchant to Alexander's father,

---

Benjamin Hawkins, 1796-1816 (Norman: University of Oklahoma Press, 1986), 3.

[2] Lawrence Kinnaird, "International Rivalry in the Creek Country: Part I. The Ascendancy of Alexander McGillivray, 1783-1789," Florida Historical Quarterly. 10 (October, 1931): 66; Arthur Preston Whitaker, "Alexander McGillivray, 1783-1789," North Carolina Historical Review. 5 (April, 1928): 191.

[3] *McGillivray* to *Panton*, August 10, 1789, John Walton Caughey, McGillivray of the Creeks (Norman: University of Oklahoma Press, 1938), 248.

Lachlan McGillivray. Panton hints at the reasons for McGillivray's impoverished condition by writing that, "I found him deserted by the British, without pay, without money, without friends, and without property, saving a few negroes".[4]

The Creek leader's indebtedness to Panton, Leslie, and Company does not fully display the reality of the political environment that existed by the middle of the 1780s. It is true that McGillivray was dependent upon Panton's Company for a steady supply of the European trade goods, which the Creek Confederacy had long grown reliant upon. The Creek Indian leader listened to the advice of, and borrowed sums of money from, the firm's head merchant William Panton.   However, the Scottish merchant realized that his trading company's prosperity ultimately rested upon the continued assistance and patronage of McGillivray. Panton remembered that it was the Spanish who controlled the nearest seaports and McGillivray's influence in the region made trade not only possible -- but profitable.[5]

Both McGillivray and Panton possessed a common interest, and it benefited them to work together in order to achieve this common interest. Both men had been financially injured during the Revolutionary War, and possessed a direct financial stake in the economic trade networks that were re-developing in the Southern backcountry of the 1780s. Their specific goals were different, but unless McGillivray and Panton cooperated on their efforts, neither goal was achievable. McGillivray, by the mid-1780s, had attained a position of high authority and influence within the multi-tribal council of the Creek Confederacy. After the signing of the Treaty of Pensacola in 1784, he was able to assure Panton's

---

[4] *Panton to Lachlan McGillivray*, April 10, 1794, Ibid, 363.

[5] Kinnaird, "Ascendancy of Alexander McGillivray, 1783-1789," 67; Whitaker, Alexander McGillivray, 1783-1789," 192; Albert Pickett, History of Alabama and Incidentally of Georgia and Mississippi. vol. 2 (Charleston: Walker and James, 1851), 430.

company safe and profitable business routes within the Spanish protected region of the Creek's territory. Panton's financial stability, and connection to English markets, provided the Creeks with a steady supply of goods as well as lines of financial credit.[6]

McGillivray's connection to Panton, Leslie, and Company allowed the rising leader to effectively control the flow of European goods within the Creek Confederacy. This in turn helped McGillivray solidify and expand his political base of support among the Creek Indians. McGillivray and Panton found themselves in a symbiotic relationship, with the mutual corporation of the two benefiting the whole. The success of McGillivray and Panton's undertaking is demonstrated with the expansion of the Panton, Leslie, and Company's trade into Pensacola by 1785, and indirectly Mobile by 1788.[7]

.   .   .   .

The relationship that the rising Creek leader developed with Spain had projected McGillivray's influence beyond the perimeters of a cultural broker. The Treaty of Pensacola had placed the Creek Confederacy under the protection of the Spanish Crown, a familiar diplomatic maneuver among southern Native American tribes. American history during the eighteenth century is riddled with numerous instances of American Indians opposing English settlers (invaders) by serving as allies for the French or Spanish monarchies. In turn, these European governments usually armed and directed their Native American allies against British interest and goals.[8] McGillivray's alliance with Spain followed this

---

[6] Mary Ann Oglesby Neeley, "Alexander McGillivray, Diplomatic Leader of the Creeks: 1783-1793," (M. A. Thes., Auburn University, 1973), 51-52.

[7] Ibid, 52; Duvon C. Corbitt ed. & tr., "Papers Relating to the Georgia-Florida Frontier, 1784-1800," Georgia Historical Quarterly 20 (December, 1936): 357.

[8] Gary B. Nash, "The Image of the Indian in the Southern Colonial Mind," William and Mary Quarterly 29 (April, 1972): 222.

eighteenth-century tradition and developed into what some scholars have termed a *patron - client* relationship.

A *patron*, as an entity, is able to distribute assets in order to gain access or control over the resources of a *client*. If the client accepts the terms offered by the patron, he or she is rewarded and protected for his or her loyalty and dependence.[9] In the 1780s, McGillivray had become a client under the patronage of Spain, with this clearly displayed in the first clause of his assigned duties as a Spanish Commissary:

> *Your first and chief duty will be to keep the different towns of your nation dependent on and subordinate to our Sovereign, using whatever means your well-known activity and talent may dictate to keep the Indians on our side.*[10]

The phrase "your well-known activity and talent" is an interesting choice of words for the Spanish government to use in describing the Creek Indian leader. Spanish officials by 1784 were already aware of McGillivray's talents and cross-cultural political and economic connections.

McGillivray's diplomatic subservience to Spain, even though it placed him in a patron - client relationship with this foreign power, provided the Creek Confederacy with valuable resources. One of the major benefits of an alliance with Spain was that it provided for the establishment of trade routes that excluded American seaports in both South Carolina and Georgia.

---

[9] Margaret Connell Szasz ed., Between Indian and White Worlds: The Cultural Broker (Norman: University of Oklahoma Press, 1994), 11-12; John H. Bodley, Cultural Anthropology: Tribes, States, And the Global System (Mountain View, California: Mayfield Publishing Company, 1994), 381.

[10] Duties under the Spanish Commission Held by Alexander McGillivray, 20 July 1784, Dorothy V. Jones, License for Empire: Colonialism by Treaty in Early America (Chicago: University of Chicago Press, 1982), 198.

McGillivray's dislike of the Americans, particularly the Georgians, has been previously mentioned, but his selection of trade alliances and routes also may have been influenced by the fact that he was skeptical of the United States' longevity as an independent nation. At one point he noted that, "the back Inhabitants of Georgia & Carolina are in arms, to oppose the Tax Collectors. The whole Continent is in Confusion. Before long I expect to hear that the three kings [England, France, and Spain] must Settle the matter by dividing America between them."[11]

Another crucial economic benefit was that the Creek Confederacy, through McGillivray's *client* relationship with Spain, received valuable "presents" from their Spanish patrons.[12] These "gifts" took the form of thousands of pounds of "powder, balls, guns, knives, and hatchets."[13] Important European trade items that the Creeks could not manufacture themselves. These gifts became an increasingly important aspect of Creek diplomacy. The Creek Confederacy in the mid-1780s, with Spanish backing, fought a series of small scale border wars with the state of Georgia. Success in these military excursions was only made possible due to the flow of Spanish weapons into the hands of Creek warriors.

Within the Congress of the newly formed United States, divergent opinions existed in regards to the official policy of Native American land reparations. Both opinions advocated for the cession of Indian territories, but the general tone of Congress was that Native Americans could remain on part of their land until the expansion of the states required additional territory. United States

---

[11] *McGillivray* to *O'Neill*, February 5, 1784, Caughey, McGillivray of the Creeks, 70.

[12] *Miro* to *McGillivray*, June 7, 1784, Ibid, 77.

[13] Talk between Zepedes the Governor of Florida and Yntipaya Masla, the principle warrior of the Lower Creek Indians, called Toclatoche, article 5, Ibid, 115; Michael D. Green, "Alexander McGillivray," In Studies in Diversity: American Indian Leaders, ed. R. David Edmunds (Lincoln: University of Nebraska Press, 1980), 53.

commissioners were ordered to establish meetings with southeastern Indian tribes in order to take into account earlier treaties, and not ratify any future treaties that were inconsistent with United States policy. However, Georgian officials possessed their own plans for territorial expansion, and the state of Georgia refused to wait for the sluggish policy-decisions of the U. S. Congress.[14] In a series of fraudulent treaties made with members of the Creek Confederacy, Georgia created two new counties on its western border. These combined treaties, Augusta (1783), Galphinton (1785), and Shoulderbone (1786), granted the state large tracks of land which soon encouraged settlement along their western border.[15]

McGillivray and the Confederacy's council members had loudly protested the territorial transfer, claiming that it was unauthorized and illegal. Surviving historical evidence supports Creek accounts that the treaties had been signed under highly questionable circumstances. For example, the Treaty of Augusta was negotiated by Creek chiefs who represented only two of the towns out of the possible thirty-four villages which were directly or indirectly affected by the treaty with the state of Georgia. To fully comprehend the dubious nature of this treat, one needs to look at the sheer size of the Creek Confederacy. During the eighteenth century there were at least thirty-nine separate clans among the Creek Indians. However, the exact size of the Creek Confederacy during this period is unknown. A map compiled by the British government around 1770 listed the number of Creek villages at forty-five. By the 1780s, there were likely as many as fifty to one

---

[14] Mary Ann Oglesby Neeley, "Alexander McGillivray, Diplomatic Leader of the Creeks: 1783-1793," (M. A. Thes., Auburn University, 1973), 53.

[15] Randolph C. Downes, "Creek-American Relations, 1782-1790," Georgia Historical Quarterly 21 (June 1937): 148-151; Thomas D. Watson, Striving for Sovereignty: Alexander McGillivray, Creek

hundred tribes, with as many as 20,000 people living within the boundaries of the Creek Confederacy.[16]

One of the chiefs who had taken part in the treaties with the Georgians later told a furious Creek council that all of the Indians present at the treaty negotiations and been, "threatened with instant death if they did not comply."[17] The chief added that, "Under such circumstances wishing to preserve their own and the company's lives -- they consented to the cession demanded, and which they knew the nations [the Confederacy] would not confirm."[18]

The surge of Georgian settlers into the disputed territory forced McGillivray to convene a special meeting of the Confederacy's Council in April, 1786. In an almost unanimous decision, the council agreed to send warriors into the disputed region in order to drive the invading Georgian settlers out. Acting in conjunction with the Cherokees to the North, Indian warriors flowed into the Cumberland Valley settlements of Tennessee, as well as into the disputed border region between the Creek Confederacy and Georgia. The warriors were under explicit orders from McGillivray to, "traverse all that part of the Country in dispute & wherever they found any American settlers to drive them off & to destroy all the buildings on it."[19] He cautioned them,

---

Warfare, and Diplomacy, 1783-1790," Florida Historical Quarterly 58 (April, 1980): 404-406.

[16] John R. Swanton, Early History of the Creek Indians and Their Neighbors (Washington: United States Government Printing Office, 1922), map attached to the inside of the back book-flap. John R. Swanton, The Indians of the Southeastern United States (Washington: United States Government Printing Office, 1946), 658-660; Thomas John Kennedy, "The Origins of Creek Indian Nationalism: Contact, Diplomacy, Clans, and Intermarriage During the Colonial and Early National Periods," (M. A. Thes., University of Houston, 1992), 129.

[17] The Tallassee King (Creek Chief) responding to the Creek Council at Tookabatcha, November, 1784, Downes, "Creek-American Relations, 1782-1790," 145.

[18] Ibid.

[19] McGillivray to Miro, may 1, 1786, Caughey, McGillivray of the Creeks, 109; Michael D. Green, "Alexander McGillivray," In

however "to conduct themselves with moderation & to shed no blood on no pretence but where self defence made it absolutely necessary. Neither were they to cross over or within the acknowledged Limits of the States."[20]

McGillivray's statement demonstrates that he possessed no wish to expand the Confederacy's territory, only to maintain the regions current boundaries. During these conflicts with the state of Georgia, and to a lesser degree South Carolina, he asked state officials to restrain their "settlers within the boundaries established and agreed upon in the year 1773, when Georgia belonged to the British government."[21] The Treaty of 1783, which had ended the American Revolution, did not recognize these earlier 1773 boundaries. Not surprisingly, Georgian officials found McGillivray's proposed boundaries too restrictive, leaving the Creek leader with few options. Creek warriors, well-supplied with Spanish weapons due to Panton's trading company, swept the disputed territory clean of American settlers.[22] Georgian settlers attempted to return during the following winter, but armed Creek warriors once again drove the invaders out during the following spring. Some surviving historical accounts state that in the Cumberland River area (present-day Tennessee) forty-two settlers were slain by these Indian attacks in 1787.[23]

The degree to which Spain played a part in the Creek Confederacy's victory was significant, but the exact amount of the Spanish aid is unknown. One historian has estimated that from

---

Studies in Diversity: American Indian Leaders, ed. R. David Edmunds, 52.

[20] Ibid.

[21] *McGillivray* to *Habersham* (President of the Georgian committee of Indian commissioners), September 18, 1786, Caughey, *McGillivray of the Creeks*, 131.

[22] *McGillivray* to *Habersham* (President of the Georgian committee of Indian commissioners), September 18, 1786, Caughey, *McGillivray of the Creeks*, 131.

June 20, 1786, to October 19, 1787, a total of 7200 pounds of gunpowder, 150 firearms, several thousand pounds of balls (bullets), as well as several hundred flints were issued to the Creek Confederacy through trading post in Pensacola as a gift from the Spanish government.[24] It is difficult to reconstruct a precise historical record of the transactions which occurred between the Spanish government and McGillivray's Creek Confederacy. The Spanish governors were subdued in their support of the Confederacy and carried out some of these patronage activities in secret.

       This secrecy is illustrated by the Spanish Governor Miro of Louisiana when he wrote to his assistant that "this matter should be handled with the greatest circumspection; therefore I hope that you will prudently find means to deliver these supplies with the fewest possible persons knowing about it." The Spanish Governor continues by suggesting that it would be "a good method to deposit this ammunition in his warehouse, so that in all events they might seem to have been bought by McGillivray." He continues by stating that the Indians should obtain their gifts "at an hour when there probably would be no one in the neighborhood to notice it." Furthermore, "the Indians should come to get them [gifts of ammunition] at different times, in order that they would appear to have been purchased by different tribes."[25] Naturally, the clandestine nature of Spain's relationship with McGillivray makes it difficult to distinguishing between legitimate purchases and outright gifts or bribes.

---

[23] Michael D. Green, "Alexander McGillivray," In Studies in Diversity: American Indian Leaders, ed. R. David Edmunds, 53; Whitaker, "Alexander McGillivray, 1783-1789," 197.

[24] Arthur Preston Whitaker, "Alexander McGillivray, 1783-1789," 196.

[25] Miro to O'Neill, June 20, 1786, Caughey, McGillivray of the Creeks, 118.

McGillivray success at repelling the American settlers only increased his prestige inside and outside of the Creek Confederacy. Georgian and South Carolinian settlers both developed a keen hatred of McGillivray, yet they were forced to acknowledge his growing political power. This lingering hatred for Alexander McGillivray, and his ordering of Creek warriors to push Americans eastward; is displayed by the fact that some contemporary historians use the term "Alexander Outlaw" to describe the Creek Indian leader.[26] However, his victory over the invading Americans would not have been possible without a steady supply of European weapons from Spanish seaports. By 1787 he was obviously in control of the Creek Confederacy, aided in part by his clientage to Spain and the trading connections with Panton, Leslie, and Company. Once again historical circumstances, much like what had occurred with his *interpreter* and *broker* positions, allowed McGillivray to expand beyond the usual circumstances of a *patron - client* relationship. A crucial element behind this expansion of influence was the American Indian leader's ability to blend economic and military principles in order to achieve the goals of the Creek Confederacy.

.   .   .   .

The trading circumstances that McGillivray had arranged within the Creek Confederacy created a sizable monopoly for the Creek leader. Every town located in the Confederacy contained a trader who was supported by Panton, Leslie, and Company. These merchants conducted all of their business transactions in the name of Panton's firm, with all trade goods flowing through the company channels. Traders who worked through Panton's company were required to possess a license which was only attained through

---

[26] Florette Henri, The Southern Indians and Benjamin Hawkins, 1796-1816, 46-47.

McGillivray.[27] Traders conducting business under McGillivray's assigned licenses were subject to a list of regulations and stipulations which, as an influential Confederacy leader, he helped to write.[28]

McGillivray was the Creek Confederacy's official Spanish commissary, which allowed him to easily regulate who sold Spanish trade goods, a fact that also assisted his rise to political power.[29] A letter from the governor of West Florida explicitly stated this point, with Spain granting McGillivray considerable, if not total, control of commerce within the Confederacy. "Therefore we order the traders and individuals of the said Creek nation to recognize him [McGillivray] as the commissary, obeying the orders which in the name of the captain general and the particular commandants of these provinces he shall give for the good of the service."[30] His recognition as a Spanish commissary, as well as a supplier of European weapons and merchandise, had placed Alexander in a very advantageous leadership position.

McGillivray's overseeing of Spanish weapons and other trade items allowed him to control the final distribution of these "gifts" to the Creek Indians. He was allowed to reward loyal Creek followers, as well as punish opposing factions within the Confederacy. As any shrewd political figure knows the limiting or outright denial of gifts or services, is also a formable display of power. This meant that Creek chiefs and towns that had aligned against McGillivray's policies, found it increasingly difficult to find traders with whom they could conduct business. In order to receive the Spanish Crown's gift of munitions, an individual needed to

---

[27] *McMurphy* to *O'Neill*, July 11, 1786, Ibid, 119.

[28] Michael D. Green, "Alexander McGillivray," In Studies in Diversity: American Indian Leaders, ed. R. David Edmunds, 51.

[29] Ibid.

[30] [*Miro*] to *McGillivray*, June 7, 1784, Caughey, McGillivray of the Creeks, 77.

possess a "paper" signed by Alexander McGillivray.[31] Any Creek Indians without access to European weapons would have a difficult time defending themselves or hunting for game.[32]

Within the Creek Confederacy, McGillivray's political position had assumed the form of a *patron*, much in the same way the Spanish government was his patron. Inside the Confederacy, McGillivray rewarded valuable resources (European goods) to political factions or individuals (clients) who were loyal to his cause. By the mid to late 1780s, the Creek leader had transformed the nature and scope of his political and economic activities.

McGillivray's patron - client relationship eventually developed a dualistic existence. At the international level he had assumed a *client* role with Spain, but within the Creek Confederacy, McGillivray had become a *patron* for numerous Creek chiefs and villages. It is from this political and economic power base that McGillivray began to re-define the structure and nature of politics within the Creek Confederacy.

McGillivray's complex rise to power has inspired past scholars to create interesting speculations about his exact political persona. To some historians he is a manipulative if not outright Machiavellian leader, whose only goal was to maximize his personal position in society. Others have compared the Scottish-Creek leader to a dictator of the Creek Nation, ruling with absolute power as "Emperor of the Creeks."[33] Other researchers see McGillivray as a courageous Native American leader, fighting to maintain the territorial sovereignty of the Creek Confederacy.

---

[31] *McMurphy* to *O'Neill*, July 11, 1786, Florette Henri, The Southern Indians, 119.

[32] Michael D. Green, "Alexander McGillivray," In Studies in Diversity: American Indian Leaders, ed. R. David Edmunds, 51.

[33] Carolyn Thomas Foreman, "Alexander McGillivray, Emperor of the Creeks," Chronicles of Oklahoma 7 (March, 129): 106; J. Leitch Wright Jr., Creeks and Seminoles: The Destruction and Regeneration of the Muscogulge People (Lincoln: University of Nebraska Press, 1986), 104.

Even the concept as to whether or not a Creek Nation ever existed as a defined political entity has created arguments and confusion.[34] This confusion is partially due to the open-ended use of terms like *nation*. In order to navigate through this confusion, the tools of an anthropologist become increasingly useful. Documents from the colonial period are riddled with the term *nation*, which at times was used inter-changeably with the word *tribe*. These descriptive terms were commonly used during European and Native American diplomatic affairs, but it is questionable as to whether both parties shared the same understanding of the terms. In modern anthropology the simplest definitions of a *nation* is, "a people with a common language, culture, and territory and who claim a common identity."[35] The Creek Confederacy under this definition was not a nation, but did possess a political identity that was recognized by other Native Americans and Europeans.[36]

Out of the three characteristics that define a nation, language, culture, and territory; the Creek Confederacy only possessed one for certain, a territory which was held in common. Within the context of language, the indigenous populations of the Southeast resided in "a linguistic melting pot."[37] However, when one of the Creek Micos (chief) was explaining his actions to the Confederacy's council the term "nations" was used.[38] In the using

---

[34] Wright, Creeks and Seminoles, 104.

[35] John H. Bodley, Cultural Anthropology: Tribes, States, and the Global System (Mountain View, California: Mayfield Publishing Company, 1994), 365; Joseph R. Strayer, On the Medieval Origins of the Modern State (Princeton, New Jersey: Princeton University Press, 1970), 89-111.

[36] John Howard Clinebell & Jim Thomson, "Sovereignty and Self-Determination: The Rights of Native Americans Under International Law," Buffalo Law Review 27 (Fall 1978): 680.

[37] Karen M. Booker, Languages of the Aboriginal Southeast (Metuchen, New Jersey: Scarecrow Press, Inc, 1991), ix.

[38] The Tallassee King (Creek Chief) responding to the Creek Council at Tookabatcha, November, 1784, Downes, "Creek-American Relations, 1782-1790," 145.

of the word in its plural form, valuable insight are gained as to the political identity of the late eighteenth-century Creek Indians. The Creek Indian chief's choice to use the word *nations*, in the plural form, to describe all of the indigenous inhabitants living within the boundaries of the Creek territory; implies a perception of separate ethnic identities.[39] The chief's notion of the Creek political system is closer to the definition of a confederacy, a union of persons, parties, or states in order to form a league; rather than a nation.

Under such a divided political system it would have been impossible for McGillivray to rule as a divinely sanctioned monarch or absolute dictator. However, by the late 1780s, the Creek Confederacy was facing considerable external pressures which were challenging the established structure of the confederacy. External threats and significant changes in the political landscape forced changes in the overall Creek society. It is possible that McGillivray drew inspiration from his father's traditions, using Scottish Highland political customs as a model. Scholars, however, need to execute caution in deciding whether activities were consciously adopted by Native American populations, or merely a historical coincidence. Many American Indian leaders during the 1760s and 1770s pursued their own unique strategies in order to survive the new political and cultural realities. Other historians have stated that "the Chief of the Creek Nation, as Alexander styled himself, is a good example of the position of the Highland Scots clan chief. It fuses both the military and civil leadership in one man who is the head of an extended organization of family and clan."[40]

---

[39] Downes, "Creek-American Relations, 1782-1790," 145.

[40] Kennedy, "Origins of Creek Nationalism," 102; Interestingly, Spanish letters claim that "mestizo sons", "are most inclined toward the whites." *O'Neill* to *Sonora*, July 11, 1787, Caughey, McGillivray of the Creeks, 157; Daniel H. Usner, Jr. Indians, Settlers, & Slaves in a Frontier Exchange Economy (Chapel Hill: University of North Carolina, 1992), 122.

More concise descriptions of the Creek political system describe it as "politically organized chiefdoms".[41] These chiefdoms were made up of societies which possessed a communal·like nature, with a central agency (a council) coordinating the necessary governmental activities. The individual chiefs, and other leaders, enjoyed high status within their respective society, but overall political and military power was limited.[42] The Creek Confederacy fits this societal model, yet it started to change under the leadership of McGillivray.[43]

The political centers within the Confederacy began to fall under the control of McGillivray. The Indian leader's control of the supply of European goods, as well as who would benefit from gifts, allowed him to partially replace the traditional coordinating agency, the Creek council. Creek villages were essentially economic in origin and function, with their political identity created from a multi·ethnic community base.[44] McGillivray had maintained the status quo of the traditional Creek tribal villages, but economically he had abandon, or at least restricted the multi·community base of the organized Creek chiefdom (the Confederacy). A multi·community base meant that politics were highly fragmented, a tribal feature which frequently troubled McGillivray. With the help of Panton's trading company and the Spanish government, he began to gather and consolidate the Confederacy's resources under the direction of one political office. The fact that one individual was able to control an increasing amount of economic and political

---

[41] One of the closest parallels to these would be the ancient city-states of Greece, Grant D. Jones & Robert R. Kauty ed., The Transition to Statehood in the New World (Cambridge: Cambridge University Press, 1981), 40; Caughey, McGillivray of the Creeks, 7.

[42] Carol R. Ember & Melvin Ember, Cultural Anthropology (Englewood Cliffs, New Jersey: Prentice Hall, 1990), 358.

[43] Jones & Kauty ed., Transition to Statehood, 43.

[44] Ibid.

power altered the structure of Creek politics, as well as shifted the entire southeast region's balance of power.

Interestingly, the Creek Confederacy did not perceive McGillivray as a chief, or in Creek Indian terminology, a *mico*. His official position in the Confederacy was that of an advisor and spokesperson to the *micos* of the head council.[45] This fact is not surprising if one remembers that McGillivray originally entered Creek politics as a cultural *interpreter* or *mediator*. His official position as an advisor and spokesperson was a leftover development from his early years of working with the British during the American Revolution. There were in fact numerous advisors and spokespersons (headmen) in the Confederacy who were given the title of "beloved men" or *isti atcagagi*. These individuals were recognized for their sound and valuable advice, which motivated tribal *micos* to give these "beloved men" a voice at Creek council meetings. The role of these individuals was to offer suggestions, state opinions, and clarify topics of interest for the councils.[46]

McGillivray's leadership position was partially an extension of the Creek tradition which had allowed knowledgeable individuals to assist the chiefs. However, Alexander's title contained a unique addition; he was not simply a beloved man, but an *isti atcagagi thlucco*, which meant "Great Beloved Man."[47] Even with the addition of "Great" to his official title, McGillivray never outwardly tampered with the official structure of the Confederacy's Council; but internal politics were altered, or at least re-structured, in order to benefit McGillivray. Historians have pointed out that much of William Panton's correspondences from this time period imply that McGillivray's action, as a spokesperson for the Treaty of

---

[45] Michael D. Green, "Alexander McGillivray," In Studies in Diversity: American Indian Leaders, ed. R. David Edmunds, 49.
[46] Ibid.
[47] Ibid.

Pensacola in 1784; created the assumption among Spanish officials that the Creek-Scottish leader was a head chief within the Confederacy. It even appears that over time most of the Creek's population also came to believe that McGillivray was a head chief. His Spanish protected patronage, as well as his control of trade within the Confederacy, generated a considerable amount of regional power and influence for the leader; which was maintained and solidified through the use of what some would call quasi-Machiavellian methods.[48]

The political methods that Alexander McGillivray employed were partially the result of his expansion of power due to his Spanish patronage. One of his duties as a Spanish Commissionary states, "You are always to exert yourself to unite the Nation in whatever course of action will promote its best interests and its glory."[49] McGillivray upheld his Spanish duties, and fully utilized the phrase "whatever course of action" to "promote" his and his supporters' "best interest". As a commissionary for the Spanish Empire, McGillivray was able to control most of the Creek Confederacy's supply of European trade goods. In particular, European made muskets, powder, and shot; which were literally the lifeblood of the Confederacy.

Other duties created from his "Commissionary" position only further emphasized McGillivray's regional influence. "You will arrest those traders who come into the Nation without posting the required bond with the Governor of Pensacola, requiring those traders who are already in the Nation to help you without the least delay. If they do not, they will be severely punished."[50] To McGillivray's benefit the Spanish had granted him power to

---

[48] Caughey, McGillivray of the Creeks, 25.
[49] Dorothy V. Jones, License for Empire: Colonialism by Treaty in Early America, 199.
[50] Ibid, 198-199.

severely punish merchants who traded outside of his economic network. As a Spanish Commissionary, his duties of office allowed him to introduce a level of threat or compulsion into the arena of Creek Indian politics. Due to his control of the economic trade channels within the Confederacy, he was able to implement European-nation style demands for loyalty.[51]

McGillivray's ruling style at times resembled the tactics of a late-nineteenth or early-twentieth century political boss. He maintained a squad of personal bodyguards who doubled as political assassins, with Georgians frequently attempting to bribe both traders and Indians to assassinate the Native American leader. However, the occurrence and use of assassinations in the southeastern region is far from a novel concept in European/Indian relations. It was simply a viable political tactic in the eighteenth-century backcountry.[52] The Georgian attempts on McGillivray life likely motivated the leader to encircle himself with trusted, able-bodied warriors. The Native American leader was well aware of these plots on his life and in a letter to Governor O'Neill he noted that, "I understand that a person is lately arrived in the Lower Towns at the Cussitahs from Georgia & he is ordered to endeavor to get somebody to Murder me privately."[53] McGillivray later learned that the Georgians "had offered four horse loads of Goods to any Indian that would procure my death."[54]

---

[51] Michael D. Green, "Alexander McGillivray," In Studies in Diversity: American Indian Leaders, ed. R. David Edmunds, 51.

[52] Ibid; Daniel H. Usner, Jr. Indians, Settlers, & Slaves, 92-93; see also Major Celeb Swan, "Position and State of Manners and Arts in the Creek, or Muscogee Nation in 1791." In Henry Rowe Schoolcraft, Historical and Statistical Information respecting the History, Conditions, and Prospects of the Indian Tribes of the United States, 6 vols. (Philadelphia: Lippincott, Grambo, & Company, 1851-57), 5:281.

[53] McGillivray to O'Neill, March, 4, 1787, Caughey, McGillivray of the Creeks, 144.

[54] McGillivray to O'Neill, April 18, 1787, Caughey, McGillivray of the Creeks, 149.

The Americans were never successful in murdering the Creek leader, which implies two general conclusions. The first is that McGillivray's power base and protection had solidified to such an extent that any assassination attempt upon his life was nearly impossible. The second observation was that perhaps he was well enough liked, at least among the majority of Indians within the Confederacy; that few wished to kill him. Both speculations are likely true since the vast majority of Creek Indians must have realized that McGillivray provided the best defense against aggressive neighbors who hungered for Creek territory. However, McGillivray's possession of a personal police force, in order to guarantee that people obeyed his policies, was also helpful.

McGillivray's use of force to maintain his authority within the Confederacy was mentioned in a personal letter to a Spanish officer. "Ever Since the Execution of Colonel Sullivan the whole white people in this nation behave remarkably well & live with the Indians very Quietly. Public examples are sometimes necessary particularly in this Country, as executing one notorious offender, oftentimes saves the lives of several."[55]

United States Major C. Swan's first-hand account of the Creek Confederacy in 1791 also mentions the execution of Colonel Sullivan. Swan states that during McGillivray's attempt to solidify his control within the Creek Confederacy, "the struggle became at last so serious, that the beloved chief had one Sullivan and two others, partizans of the micos, put to death in the public squares. They were all three white men who had undertaken to lead the faction against him; but he finally crushed the insurgents, and effected his purposes."[56] Swan continues by stating that

---

[55] *McGillivray to O'Neill*, January 3, 1784, Ibid, 66-67.

[56] Major Celeb Swan, "Position and State of Manners and Arts in the Creek, or Muscogee Nation in 1791." In Henry Rowe Schoolcraft, Historical and Statistical Information respecting the History, Conditions, and Prospects of the Indian Tribes of the

McGillivray's personal assistants or bodyguards were comprised of "several active warriors. . . whom the chief keeps continually attached to him by frequent and profuse presents," and "often in the capacity of constables·· pursue, take up, and punish, such characters as he may direct; and on some occasions have acted as executioners."[57]   Interestingly, Major Swan also describes McGillivray as a "chief" and not as a "beloved man" or an advisor.

On at least five occasions Alexander McGillivray used the act of assassination to obtain his political ends; with four of the attempted killings being successful.   Every victim was white (European/American), with three of them deeply involved in Creek politics and supporting objectives which were in direct opposition to the McGillivray's policies.   The execution of these individuals seriously weakened the anti-McGillivray faction within the Confederacy and bolstered his political position.[58]   At first glance this use of heavy-handed techniques appears overly harsh, but within the context of the region, as well as the eighteenth century, these actions are more justifiable.   This is especially true when viewed along with works such as St. John Crevecoeur 1783 published travel accounts of the new created United States of America. In his writings the author, veteran of the earlier French and Indian war and a naturalized American citizen, bluntly describes "the backsettlers of both the Carolinas, Virginia, and many other parts."   He notes that they "have been long a set of lawless people; it has been even dangerous to travel among them."

United States, 6 vols. (Philadelphia: Lippincott, Grambo, & Company, 1851-57), 5:281.

[57] Ibid, 5:282.

[58] Michael D. Green, "Alexander McGillivray," In Studies in Diversity: American Indian Leaders, ed. R. David Edmunds, 51.

Crevecoeur even states that "what a detestable idea such people must have given to the natives of the European!"[59]

McGillivray's position as a *client* under Spanish *patronage*, allowed for a considerable range of command within the Creek Confederacy; yet his control was not absolute. The use of assassination as a political tool possessed definite limits in McGillivray's diplomatic maneuverings. For example, no historical evidence exists to suggest that the aspiring leader ever murdered another Creek Indian. The killing of an outsider was bearable, but such an act directed against a fellow Creek was intolerable and not allowed under Creek customs.[60] If it had not been for this established Creek tradition, the Creek-Scot leader may have added two Creek *micos* to his list of assassination victims.

The limit of McGillivray's influence was also displayed by the presence of a small pro-American faction within the Confederacy. During the American Revolution this faction had resisted numerous attempts to construct a focused anti-American/pro-British political and military position. In later years, individual *micos* from this faction, ignoring McGillivray's advice and warnings, acted on their own to make controversial treaties with the Americans. Alexander displayed his annoyance when he referred to a Creek Indian *mico* known as Tame King, "who is well known to be but a roving beggar, going wherever he thinks he can get presents."[61] A letter from 1786 to Spanish officials demonstrates McGillivray's anger over the fragmented leadership structure of the Confederacy. After citing the "ungenerous,

---

[59] J. Hector St. John Crevecoeur, Letters form an American Farmer (London: John Davis, 1782; reprint, Gloucester, Massachusetts: Peter Smith, 1968), 60.

[60] Michael D. Green, "Alexander McGillivray," In Studies in Diversity: American Indian Leaders, ed. R. David Edmunds, 51.

[61] *McGillivray* to *O'Neill*, February 10, 1786, Caughey, McGillivray of the Creeks, 103.

Cowardly & treacherous Intentions" of the Georgians, the young
Creek leader continued by stating that:

> We [the Creeks] cannot boast of being perfectly clean
> ourselves, there are a few of Note as the Tallassie King &
> Fat King. . . that have been long in the American Interest,
> forwarding their Views against this Country, on which
> account I lament that our Customs, (unlike those of
> Civilized people) Won't permit us to treat [them] as traitors
> by giving them the usual punishment.[62]

In this situation, McGillivray felt that the two micos had
committed treason against the Creek Confederacy by courting
American favors.   The Tallassie King, also known as *Hoboithle
Mico*, and the Fat King or *Eneah Mico* had both violated his orders
and attended treaty negotiations with the Georgians in 1785 and
1786. They had signed the Treaty of Galphinton and the Treaty of
Shoulder-Bone, without the consensus of the overall Creek
Confederacy's leadership council.   McGillivray felt that the
punishment of death should have been imposed upon the rogue
micos, but he was forced to accept the destruction of the Tallassie
King's house, crops, horses, and cattle.[63]

McGillivray's frustration with both the "Tallassie King"
and the "Fat King" demonstrated the complexity of politics and
tribal traditions in the Creek Confederacy. The fragmented nature
of the Southeastern backcountry (the old southwest) allowed for
numerous, at times conflicting, cultural interactions; which

---

[62] *McGillivray* to *Zepedes*, November 15, 1786, Ibid, 139.
[63] Michael D. Green, "Alexander McGillivray," In Studies in
Diversity: American Indian Leaders, ed. R. David Edmunds, 51-
52; Linda Grant De Pauw ed., Senate Executive Journal and Related
Documents vol. 2 (Baltimore: Johns Hopkins University Press,
1974), 165; Swan, "State of Manners," In Schoolcraft, Indian

sometimes created conditions that produced social and political instability. McGillivray's definition of treason, as well as his interpretation of governmental authority, ultimately conflicted with the traditional Creek Indian understanding of the concept. Creek Indians did not possess a code of written laws, but they did have an established set of customs, procedures, and practices. However, not all Native American practices matched up to European concepts of a formal jurisprudence, which was a fact that Alexander was forced to reconcile with as he gained political and economic power.[64]

The Creek-Scot leader could only alter the structure of the Confederacy's government to a degree, which is demonstrated by his inability to fully punish the two pro-American Creek *micos*. With more time, perhaps, he could have fully transformed the Creek Confederacy into an organized nation state (similar to European traditions), but time was a luxury that even his influence could not control. Even with these setbacks, McGillivray was able to solidify his power base and eventually expanded from the boundaries of a cultural *broker*, into the more complex arena of *patron-client* relationships. Even though the Creek leader had assumed the role of a *client* under Spanish patronage, this did not mean that he ceased to act as a powerful cultural *broker*. The *client-patron* relationship became effectively superimposed upon his original *brokerage* activities, with a new leadership identity emerging by the late 1780s. McGillivray had become an influential *patron*, while the Creek Confederacy assumed the role of a *client* who was dependent upon his access to trade goods.

·   ·   ·   ·

Established business alliances, as well as parental kinship connections, provided Alexander McGillivray with substantial

Tribes, 5:282; It is not known whether any action was taken against the Fat King.
[64] Joseph J. Thompson, "Law Amongst the Aborigines of the Mississippi Valley," Illinois Law Quarterly 6 (December 1923): 204.

benefits. The triangle of influence created between the Creek Indian leader, Panton, Leslie & Company, as well as the Spanish Crown; placed McGillivray in an advantageous position. Spain's protection of the pre-existing trade networks, with trade conducted out of Panton's stores, forced the trading company to rely on McGillivray's influence within the Confederacy. McGillivray's courting of Spanish protection provided opportunities for considerable political and diplomatic maneuvering. The definition of a mere cultural *broker* had become far too constraining of a term to fully describe McGillivray's actions and expanding influence.

McGillivray had pursued a *patron-client* relationship with Spain, which was soon tested by the invasion of Georgian settlers into the eastern borders of the Creek Confederacy. However, Creek warriors from the Confederacy conducted a successful defense of their borders, largely due to the steady supply of ammunitions obtained through Spanish ports. With the Americans forced to retreat, McGillivray began to develop a more dynamic range of influence within the Southeast. Through a mixture of political and economic power, he attempted to restructure the internal political organization of the Confederacy; while leaving the outward structure virtually untouched.

The American Indian leader's policies displayed the potentially violent nature of the region's politics. McGillivray's attempt to create a unified Creek nation, while solidify power and politically redefining some Creek political customs; were met by dissenters who purposely went against his wishes. Aggressive American settlers, intrusive merchants, and independently-minded *micos* were a direct reflection of the southeastern region's political complexity; all of which hindered McGillivray's attempt to reorganize the Confederacy. However, even with these difficulties, McGillivray was able to develop a center of political power and expand the traditional definition of a *patron - client* relationship.

Chapter 5

♦

Cultural Coalescence: A Dynamic World View, 1790 - 1793

Spain's patron support of Alexander McGillivray as a client began to waver by the late 1780s. His influential power base, as well as extensive hostilities between the Americans and the Creek Confederacy, motivated the Spanish to become less generous with their assignment of presents and privileges to the Creek Indians. The cooling in relations between the Spanish and the Creek Confederacy drove the young leader to search for new diplomatic relationships and solutions. This search took the form of accepting treaty overtures from the United States' newly formed federal government, which was now operating under a recently adopted constitution.

The acceptance of the U. S. government's overtures led to the signing in 1790 of the Treaty of New York, a treaty which carried profound implications for both the United States and the Creek Confederacy. The treaty set a precedent by expanding the influence of the Federal government, while greatly diminishing the individual diplomatic powers of the individual states. The Treaty of New York allowed McGillivray to recreate many of the agreements and privileges which had been part of the 1784 Treaty of Pensacola. These political actions in 1790 displayed a level of flexible and pragmatic thinking that many other leaders could not have accomplished. McGillivray's life lessons had long ago taught him that the source of a solution was of lesser importance than its overall end result.

McGillivray's mutable view of politics and diplomacy seems to imply that he possessed a questionable level of personal ethics and loyalty. On the contrary, this blending or *coalescence* of past positions, relationships, and experiences did not simply create a superb opportunist; rather his actions demonstrated a more holistic, broader world view of politics and diplomacy. These abilities become quite evident when exploring certain key events from the Creek-Scot leader's life.

McGillivray continually strove to achieve a sense of Creek Indian independence and territorial sovereignty. The survival solutions that he promoted were, in many ways, different from those advanced by other famous Native American resistance leaders. The mystic approach of original tribal purity, which motivated figures like the Ottawa chief Pontiac and the charismatic Shawnee leader Tecumseh, were never part of McGillivray's vocabulary. His remedies for the Confederacy's besieged borders arose from ideas which contained highly progressive and practical solutions. Foreign elements and ideals can provide an intellectual stimulus to any existing culture, with past solutions inspiring thoughtful exploration; something that McGillivray thoroughly understood. In other words, the source of an answer did not matter, just so it provided an achievable solution. This creation of a cultural *coalescence* of ideas and responses embodied McGillivray's later life. This pragmatic blending of ideas created a dynamic understanding of his political environment, which provided some level of success in slowing the territorial encroachment of the United States.

.   .   .   .

By late 1787, Alexander McGillivray was able to halt the western expansion of Georgia, largely due his diplomatic connections in with the Spanish government in Pensacola and St. Augustine. The Creek Confederacy's victories had not only forced Georgia to acknowledge their western neighbor's territorial sovereignty, but motivated the state, as well as neighboring Tennessee; to offer handsome bribes to McGillivray in an attempt to buy his friendship. The success of the *Great Beloved Man* was also circulated among Native American councils from the Choctaws (formerly located in present-day Mississippi, Alabama and Louisiana) to the Mohawks (formerly located in present-day New York and Vermont).[1] The Spanish, however, were developing a different view of McGillivray and his successes.

By the late 1780s, McGillivray had become too successful and influential for the mere *client* role that Spain had assigned him. As a *client* in a *patron-client* relationship, the Native American leader's political authority possessed definable diplomatic limits. McGillivray, however, began to push beyond the customary relationship of subservience to a Spanish *patron*. After the American Revolution, the Creek Confederacy was initially seen as a pawn by the Spanish government. As Spain struggled to maintain its colonial holdings in southeast, the Creeks were seen as a convenient ally and weapon. The Confederacy's warriors were readily armed and served as an effective buffer against the newly recognized United States. The Spanish government assumed that McGillivray, and most of the Creek Confederacy, had been inexpensively purchased with a commissary's salary and a few trade privileges. However, his rapid increase in prestige and

---

[1] Michael D. Green, "Alexander McGillivray," In Studies in Diversity: American Indian Leaders, ed. R. David Edmunds (Lincoln: University of Nebraska Press, 1980), 53; *McGillivray to O'Neill*, March 28, 1788, John Walton Caughey, McGillivray of the Creeks (Norman: University of Oklahoma Press, 1938), 172-173.

influence threatened Spain's laboriously constructed balance of power in the Southeast. They had never planned for the Creek leader to become a major player in the diplomatic power structure of the southeastern region.[2]

Spain's apprehension over McGillivray's growing political influence was evident in a letter from 1787 between the Spanish governors of East and West Florida. "McGilbray [has] become such an authority in the nation that he could bring about the entire independence of the Indians."[3] This sentence alone demonstrates the fact that McGillivray's *patron-client* relationship with the Spanish had grown beyond Spain's original patronage intentions. The letter continues by stating that if McGillivray was able to obtain full independence for the Creek Confederacy, pre-revolution English-Scot loyalties would likely emerge. "I am sure that should he succeed in this matter he would prove more loyal to the British trade than to the Spaniards."[4]   Even to Spanish officials, McGillivray's strong British (Scottish) connections were no secret.

Spanish governors also correctly predicted that "given more time [sic] he would consider himself chief of the Indian nations and independent, even though he has cooperated effectively to drive out the Americans."[5] The Spanish officer's mentioning of McGillivray possessing more loyalty "to the British trade than to the Spaniards" readily demonstrates the stubborn persistence of British sympathies in the Creek-Scot leader's trade dealings. Britain was still the primary supplier of trade goods within the Confederacy, sold by way of Panton, Leslie, and Company. The

---

[2] Michael D. Green, "Alexander McGillivray," In Studies in Diversity: American Indian Leaders, ed. R. David Edmunds, 53.
[3] O'Neill to Miro, May 21, 1787, Caughey, McGillivray of the Creeks, 153.
[4] Ibid.
[5] Ibid.

governors of East and West Florida had also started to realize that their *client* Indian leader possessed an agenda of his own.

The governors of Florida clearly understood that McGillivray's alliance with the Spanish Crown was largely a diplomatic gesture made out of political necessity. While they acknowledge that, "he has been most useful thus far in gaining for us the friendship of the Creeks," they also recognized that McGillivray "lives at an extremity of the nations, where as a mestizo he is chief of a town, and one must consider that his efforts will always be directed toward the ends that he conceives to favor the Indians his tribesmen."[6] Therefore, they believed his loyalty to Spain would always remain secondary in nature.

McGillivray's pro-Creek Indian identity and political influence was not the only motivating factor behind Spain's uneasiness with the Confederacy. The growing military presence of the United States had also begun to raise concerns for the Spanish in their controlled territories of East and West Florida. By the late 1780s, Spain had no wish to start a war with the former British colonies. McGillivray's border conflicts with Georgia threatened to create a war with the entire United States rather than just an individual state. Spanish letters from 1787 clearly acknowledge this concern: "If they [the Creeks] exasperate the Georgians with new hostilities all the states will make common cause. I think the Creeks would not be able to resist them."[7] McGillivray had echoed the same concern in October 1786, informing the Spanish governor of East Florida that the Creek Confederacy had been forced, "to make a truce with the Cumberland [Tennessee settlers] & over Mountain [white settlers or Cherokee?] people, otherwise at this time we Should have run the risk to have been attacked on two

---

[6] *O'Neill* to *Sonora*, February 20, 1787, Caughey, <u>McGillivray of the Creeks</u>, 144.

[7] *Miro* to *O'Neill*, March 24, 1787, Ibid, 145-146.

quarters at once & probably have had our Country over run & totally destroyed."[8]

McGillivray's political and economic growth beyond the traditionally accepted definition of a *client*, as well as the threat of a war with the United States; created a cooling effect in Spanish-Creek Indian relations. What had been a steady supply of Spanish gifts was starting to dwindle, and McGillivray's found his beloved Confederacy in the same predicament that had occurred when Britain had ceased its supply of trade goods in 1783. A letter from McGillivray to the Spanish on October, 1787, directly mentions that the gifts of munitions were no longer as plentiful within the Creek Confederacy. "It cannot be the Intention of Government [Spain] at this time, after having encouraged me to resist the encroaching disposition of the Americans, to withdraw its Support."[9] The Creek Indian leader must have noticed the eerie resemblance to the Confederacy's 1783 dilemma, when it suffered from a shortage of European weaponry following British withdrawal from the Southeast.[10]

In 1789, Spain renewed its support for the Creek Confederacy, but its restriction of supplies had demonstrated to McGillivray the vulnerability of his position. The wavering of Spanish support in 1787 and 1788 was Spain's way of reminding their Creek-Scot *client* of his subservience to the Spanish monarchy. The Creek leader realized that the Confederacy was at the mercy of any Spanish imperial whim. The Spanish governors wished for McGillivray to remember that they were his *patrons*, and ultimately possessed the final word on politics, economics, and diplomacy within the Creek Confederacy.

---

[8] *McGillivray* to *O'Neill*, October 30, 1786, Ibid, 135.
[9] *McGillivray* to *Zepedes*, October 6, 1787, Ibid, 163.
[10] See Chapter three, 6-7.

McGillivray was fully aware of the Spanish restrictions upon his actions, and even mentioned his disapproval of Spain's actions in letters to the Florida governors. "I trust that we [the Creek Confederacy] shall never be exposed to the risk of last year, when at the moment that our adversaries [the Americans] were making the most vigorous efforts you refused to give us any more aid or support and told us to make peace."[11] In the same letter, McGillivray openly questioned Spain's wisdom in encouraging the Confederacy to restrict their border hostilities with the Americans. "Permit me to call to your attention that if we are really forced the make peace with the Americans, they will take every advantage of our situation."[12] The Creek leader clearly was not satisfied with his patron-client relationship to the Spanish crown.

The Creek Confederacy's problems with Spain forced McGillivray to search for new diplomatic solutions. The Americans were still demanding that the Creek Indians honor the treaties of Augusta (1783), Galphinton (1785), and Shoulderbone (1786); even though all three were considered invalid by the Confederacy's tribal council.[13] He knew that a key factor for the Creek's military success against the Georgians by the mid-1780s was, in part, due to the fact that the state of Georgia received no military assistance from the newly formed federal government. The independent spirit of the former British colonies, as well as their financial poverty; was a temporary benefit for McGillivray's cause.

Furthermore, the United States possessed no unified national policy in regard to its western borders. The new federal government of the United States, under the Articles of Confederation, provided the nation with only a vaguely defined, all-

---

[11] *McGillivray* to *Miro*, August 10, 1789, Caughey, McGillivray of the Creeks, 245.
[12] Ibid.

encompassing control of North American Indian affairs; while severely limiting the actually authority of the federal government. The Articles of Confederation's ambiguity is aptly displayed in article number IX which states that the Federal Government shall possess, "the sole and exclusive right and power of . . . regulating the trade and managing all affairs with the Indians, not members of any states, provided, that the legislative right of any state within its own limits be not infringed of violated."[14]

The inability of the United States government to supply Georgia with military resources had allowed McGillivray to effectively halt the state's westward expansion. However, the establishment of a federal government under the newly ratified U. S. constitutional would greatly increase Georgia's military potential, due to the fact that the state would possess the capability to call upon a unified, national military force (the U.S. Army). In fact, the opportunity for Georgia to gain much needed federal aid was likely one of the strongest reasons behind the state's agreement to ratify the new U. S. constitution. McGillivray's letters to Spanish officials openly acknowledge this fear, "They [the Georgians] meant to obtain the Sanction of Congress to engage the whole Union in the quarrel", using "the force of the Union. . . to reduce us to accept. . . their own terms of peace."[15]

Once again, Alexander McGillivray found the Creek Confederacy in a precarious situation. Both the United States and the Spanish government were encouraging McGillivray to recognize

---

[13] For information on these treaties refer to, chapter four, "Alexander McGillivray as a Leader: From 'Broker' to a 'Patron-Client' Relationship," 7-8.

[14] Worthington C. Ford, et al, ed., Continental Congress, Journals of the Continental Congress, 1774-1789 vol. IX (Washington: United States Government Printing Office, 1907), 919; Michael D. Green, "Alexander McGillivray," In Studies in Diversity: American Indian Leaders, ed. R. David Edmunds, 54.

[15] McGillivray to Miro, August 12, 1788, Caughey, McGillivray of the Creeks, 193; Randolph C. Downes, "Creek-American

the three treaties that Georgia had made with the Creek Confederacy from 1783 to 1786. The Native American's solution to this diplomatic conundrum again revealed his shrewd ability to recognize, re-shuffle, and connect previously unrelated elements. McGillivray's creative answer to this problem propelled him to the pinnacle of his leadership career, and displayed an ability to blend seemingly opposing political and cultural forces into what can only be described as a *cultural coalescence*.

McGillivray seized upon a crucial phrase within the original Articles of Confederation. The fact that only the United States government could officially negotiate treaties and "not members of any state," provided an answer to the Confederacy's dilemma. The United States' emergence as a viable political power on the North American continent meant that Spain's influence would likely diminish. A treaty with the United States would out-maneuver the land-grabbing schemes of Georgia while gaining federal recognition (and hopefully protection) of the Creek Confederacy. By 1789, the Creek Indian leader realized that an official treaty with the newly reorganized U. S. federal government would effectively deny Georgia any future treaty ambitions. Federal protection of Creek Indian territory would essentially make Georgia diplomatically impotent.[16]

. . . .

Negotiations with the U. S. Federal government began on August, 1789, within the confines of the Creek Confederacy. The meetings were a grand occasion with numerous southern Indian tribe representatives present, with estimates ranging as high as three thousand Confederacy members in attendance during the negotiations. According to George Washington, all of the present

---

Relations, 1782-1790," Georgian Historical Quarterly 21 (June 1937): 172.
[16] Michael D. Green, "Alexander McGillivray," In Studies in Diversity: American Indian Leaders, ed. R. David Edmunds, 54.

tribes were directly or indirectly under the guidance of, "their famous Counselor, the noted McGill[i]vray."[17] Washington's words display the immense influence that the Creek Indian leader had developed by the late 1780s. Alexander was clearly more than a simple pawn in the Spanish government's diplomatic maneuvering within the Southeast.

Interestingly, representatives from both the United States and Georgia indignantly demanded that any new treaty would have to recognize Georgia's previous land claims from the earlier treaties made during the 1780s. In addition, every member of the Confederacy was to "acknowledge the Creeks to be under the protection of the United States, and of no other Sovereign whosoever; and also that they are not to hold any Treaty with any State whatsoever."[18] The granting of exclusive territorial and protective rights to the United States would have nullified any protection from Spain's 1784, Treaty of Pensacola. Because of these unfavorably demands, McGillivray and the Creek Confederacy, finding no compensation for such a one-sided treaty; broke off negotiations with the Americans and refused any further discussion.[19] The Creek Indian leader's disgust with the overall proceedings was clearly evident in his letter to William Panton. "The arts of flattery, ambition and intimidation were exhausted in

---

[17] *George Washington to Benjamin Lincoln*, August 11, 1789, John C. Fitzpatrick ed., The Writings of George Washington vol. 30 (Washington: United States Government Printing Office, 1939), 379.

[18] *McGillivray to Panton*, October 8, 1789, Caughey, McGillivray of the Creeks, 252; Lucille Griffith, Alabama: A Documentary History to 1900 (Alabama: University of Alabama Press, 1968), 47.

[19] Lucia Burk Kinnaird, "The Rock Landing Conference of 1789," North Carolina Historical Review 9 (October 1932): 349-365; Michael D. Green, "Alexander McGillivray," In Studies in Diversity: American Indian Leaders, ed. R. David Edmunds, 54.

vain. I at last told him by G···· I would not have such a Treaty cram'd down my throat."[20]

However, the U. S. federal government still wished to pursue talks with McGillivray; so in spring of 1790, President George Washington sent a special envoy to negotiate a new treaty. The federal messenger, Marinus Willett, carried "a letter of introduction to M[c]'Gillivray, blending with other subjects, a strong representation of the miseries which a war with the United States would bring upon his [McGillivray's] people", as well as "an earnest exhortation to repair, with the chiefs of his nation, to the seat of the federal government, in order to effect a solid and satisfactory peace."[21] McGillivray accepted Washington's offer and, accompanied by over two dozen Creek Indian leaders, traveled to New York in the summer of 1790.[22]

McGillivray must have realized that a trip to New York, the United States' capital, could potentially place all existing arrangements between the Creek Confederacy, Panton's trading company, and Spain in jeopardy. McGillivray had become a prominent figure within the southeast region, which by the late 1780s, had Spain needing his support just as much as the Confederacy needed Spanish support. Spain had tried to control him by withdrawing their gifts of war materials, but this only

---

[20] *McGillivray to Panton*, October 8, 1789, Caughey, McGillivray of the Creeks, 253.

[21] William M. Willett, A Narrative of the Military Actions of Colonel Marinus Willett, Taken Chiefly from His Own Manuscript (New York: G. & C. & H. Carvill, 1831; reprint, New York: New York Times and Arno Press, 1969), 95; Julian P. Boyd ed., The Papers of Thomas Jefferson vol. 17 (Princeton, New Jersey: Princeton University Press, 1965), 290.

[22] Willett, Military Actions of Colonel Marinus Willett, 103-113; Michael D. Green, "Alexander McGillivray," In Studies in Diversity: American Indian Leaders, ed. R. David Edmunds, 55.

reinforced McGillivray's desire to seek new political and economic connections.[23]

The city of New York, after the adoption of the Constitution, had become the political center of the fledgling United States. The new capital was swarming with government officials, members of congress, and numerous foreign diplomats. It was in this politically charged climate that almost thirty Creek Indian leaders, along with Alexander McGillivray, entered into talks with Washington and his Secretary of War, Henry Knox.[24]

The negotiations were initially started through a series of informal meetings held between McGillivray and Knox. After all points had been fully addressed, the final treaty was drafted and Knox was appointed as the regular treaty commissioner. The drafting of what became known as the Treaty of New York was finished by August 7th, with the official signing ceremony occurring the following week. The Treaty of New York (1790), as well as the Treaty of Fort Harmar (1789) in the Ohio Territory, would set the legal precedent for all future United States and Native American negotiations; as well as answer unresolved questions within the Federal Constitution. The Treaty of New York was also the first treaty that was negotiated and signed on non-Indian occupied land.[25]

The politically charged climate surrounding the treaty negotiations possessed an international flair, with various European interests competing for McGillivray's influence; which displays his importance as a political figure. The Spanish Empire

---

[23] Mary Ann Oglesby Neely, "Alexander McGillivray, Diplomatic Leader of the Creeks," (M. A. Thes., Auburn University, 1973), 91.

[24] J. Leitch Wright Jr., "Creek-American Treaty of 1790: Alexander McGillivray and The Diplomacy of The Old Southwest," Georgia Historical Quarterly 21 (December 1967): 379.

[25] Caughey McGillivray of the Creeks, 43; Francis Paul Prucha, The Great Father: The United States Government and the American Indians (Lincoln: University of Nebraska Press, 1984), 52.

had sent an officer by the name of Carlos Howard from St. Augustine, who informed American officials that he was merely visiting New York on sick leave. The British also took an interest in the Creek leader's visit to the U. S. capitol, sending representatives, George Beckwith and Thomas Dalton, to "witness" the proceedings.[26] The Americans, fearful that McGillivray's opinions would be unduly influenced, closely chaperoned the Creek delegation. The arrival of the Spanish agent particularly troubled United States officials, with Alexander Hamilton noting that, "we are by no means satisfied with the conduct of the Spanish Officer, who arrived lately from the foreign possessions of that Crown; we cannot prove it positively, but have every reason to think, that he has been using endeavors to check or even to frustrate our negotiations with the Creek Indians."[27]

The presence of British and Spanish agents appeared to have no direct effect upon the final treaty. But indirectly, the presence of foreign agents perhaps persuaded American officials to grant more favorable terms to the visiting Creek delegation. The United States was still a fairly fragmented and vulnerable nation, with each state still seeing itself as a sovereign entity. For example, during and immediately after the American Revolution, every state from Pennsylvania and to the north had abolished slavery; yet slavery remained intact to the south. New Englanders in the north were increasingly at odds with the proposal of limited federal government, while the southern states viewed agricultural production and slavery as an inseparable concept. Only four years earlier, in 1786, Daniel Shay's "tax" rebellion army had been put

---

[26] Harold C. Syrett ed. and Cooke, Jacob E. ed., The Papers of Alexander Hamilton vol. 6 (New York: Columbia University Press, 1962) 549.

[27] *Hamilton's* conversation with *George Beckwith* (a British agent), August 7-12, 1790, Harold C. Syrett ed., The Papers of Alexander Hamilton vol. 6 (New York: Columbia University Press, 1962) 547.

down with military force. Shay, as well as many of his followers, had been veterans of the Revolutionary War and to American leaders like Washington and Knox, represented the most dangerous aspect of democracy -- an armed and angry mob. The last thing the young nation needed were western Indian populations allied with, and armed by, European monarchs.[28]

During the treaty negotiations, Knox repeatedly attempted to create agreements that would allow for American trade, instead of Spanish; within the Creek Confederacy's borders. McGillivray, however, remained loyal to the economic network created through his Spanish patronage and William Panton's trading company. The only concession that he gave to Knox was for an arrangement of emergency trade with the United States in case pre-existing Spanish channels closed. The agreement to consent to United States trade routes and merchants during emergencies was placed in one of the many secret articles which were attached to the treaty. Another secret article from the treaty included a provision that commissioned McGillivray as an American brigadier general with an annual salary of $1200.[29]

Washington's rationale for wishing to grant McGillivray a military rank was actually noted in 1789, a year before the treaty signing. "Mr. McGillivray possesses a Commission of Colonel or Lieutenant Colonel from the King of Spain. If he could be induced to resign that Commission by the offer of one, a grade higher, the offer ought to be made and substantiated."[30] The Creek leader's resourcefulness is displayed by the fact that as a former British officer, an officially recognized Spanish colonel; he was able to

---

[28] Caughey McGillivray of the Creeks,   43.

[29] Ibid, 44; James Schouler, History of the United States of America, Under the Constitution (New York: Dodd, Mead & Company Publishers, 1880), 172.

[30] Instructions to the Commissioners for Southern Indians [from George Washington], August 29, 1789, Linda Grant De Pauw ed.,

attain the position of a U. S. brigadier general. These military positions to an outsider would, at least initially, seem to conflict with each other, but in the world of Alexander McGillivray; they were all quite possible.

The motivations for these secret articles were first suggested by George Washington, who believed the articles would increase the bargaining power of the United States. Washington stated that,

in preparing the Articles of this treaty the present arrangements of the trade with the Creeks have caused much embarrassment. It seems to be well ascertained that the said trade is almost exclusively in the hands of a company of British Merchants, who by agreement make their importation of Goods from England into the Spanish ports.[31]

Not surprisingly, the United States was uneasy about a neighboring Indian confederacy, which had a history of animosity toward Americans; receiving shipments of goods (weapons) from European interest. Washington realized, as Britain and Spain had, that "the trade of the Indians is a main mean of their political management."[32] Washington, like McGillivray, understood that trade and political stability were factors that were thoroughly entwined. The first president of the United States noted that "it is therefore obvious that the United States cannot possess any security for the performance of treaties with the Creeks, while their

---

Senate Executive Journal and Related Documents vol. II (Baltimore: Johns Hopkins University Press, 1974), 205.

[31] *Washington* to the *Senate*, August 4, 1790, Fitzpatrick, The Writings of George Washington vol. 31, 74.

[32] Ibid.

trade is liable to be interrupted or withheld at the caprice of two foreign powers."[33]

George Washington was not an idealistic statesman like Thomas Jefferson, or a philosophically inspired scholar of the abstract such as James Madison. His previous occupations as a land surveyor, engineer, army general, and plantation owner had created an individual who was motivated by practical outcomes and tangible goals. Washington, a pragmatic man, realized that the only way to ensure a successful treaty with McGillivray and the Creeks was to match Spain's offer.[34] The Treaty of New York was considered an essential instrument for achieving peace along the borders of the various southern states. A letter to the Senate from President Washington expressed this belief that, "the treaty with the Creeks may be regarded as the main foundation of the southwestern frontier of the United States."[35] Washington, the ever practical politician, likely viewed the secret articles with little concern; the overarching goal was to produce a treaty would create a more politically stable backcountry. The secret article that allowed McGillivray's Creeks to annually import sixty thousand dollars' worth of British trade goods, duty free, through any American port; meant that the Creek leader's trade monopoly was now fully sanctioned and supported by the United States' Federal Government.[36]

Washington's acceptance of these secret articles is not surprising, but its approval by the President's fellow Virginian

---

[33] Ibid.

[34] For a deeper understanding of Washington's personality and philosophy towards the western border region see, Bernhard Knollenberg, George Washington: The Virginia Period, 1732-1775 (Durham, North Carolina: Duke University Press, 1964); Wiley Sword, President Washington's Indian War: The Struggle for the Old Northwest, 1790-1795 (Norman: University of Oklahoma Press, 1985).

[35] Washington to the Senate, August 4, 1790, Fitzpatrick, The Writings of George Washington vol. 31, 88.

[36] Washington to the Senate, August 4, 1790, Ibid, 75.

Thomas Jefferson is interesting. Jefferson endorsed the ratification of the Treaty of New York, even though it continued, and legally sanctioned, the monopolistic trade network of McGillivray, Panton's Company, and the Spanish Governors. Jefferson noted that McGillivray, "having hitherto enjoyed a monopoly of the commerce of the Creek nation, with a right of importing their goods, duty-free, and considering these privileges as the principal sources of his power over that nation, is unwilling to enter into treaty with us, unless they can be continued to him."[37]

Jefferson clearly acknowledged McGillivray's tremendous influence within the Creek Confederacy, as well as the Indian leader's control of regional trade. The Virginian politician realized that such a trade arrangement with the Confederacy was not consistent with United States trade laws and regulations. This motivated Jefferson to ask the question, "how this may be done consistently with our laws, and so as to avoid just complaints from those of our citizens who would wish to participate of the trade?"[38]

Jefferson's legal solution to the treaty's secret articles was to state that the United States would commit a great diplomatic mistake if it did not enter into support with McGillivray's monopoly. He grudgingly acknowledged that American citizens "at this time, are not permitted to trade in that nation."[39] However, the next line of Jefferson's letter displays an open-minded view of national sovereignty and actually defends the rights of the Creek Confederacy. "The nation has a right to give us their peace, and to withhold their commerce, to place it under what monopolies or regulations they please. If they [the Creeks] insist that only Colo.

---

[37] Opinion on McGillivray's Monopoly of Commerce with Creek Indians, July 29, 29, 1790, Julian P. Boyd ed., The Papers of Thomas Jefferson vol. 17 (Princeton, New Jersey: Princeton University Press, 1965), 288.
[38] Ibid.
[39] Ibid.

Mc.Gillivray and his company shall be permitted to trade among them, we have no right to say the contrary."[40]

Jefferson also noted that, "we shall even gain some advantage in substituting citizens of the U. S. instead of British subjects, as associates of Colo. McGillivray, and excluding both British and Spaniards from tha[t] country."[41] Jefferson's reasoning portrays the compromising ability of an astute politician who, like McGillivray, realized that the ends can justify the means. The Treaty of New York meant a monopoly of trade that excluded Georgians and other Americans, but was fully sanctioned by the United States government.

Some scholars have argued that Jefferson's support of McGillivray's monopoly was an acknowledgment of the Confederacy's independent sovereignty. If this was the case, the Secretary of State's political position on the treaty was consistent with his views that the treaty was simply a legal recognition of Creek territorial sovereignty; over which the American federal government possessed no direct control. Other researchers have argued that Jefferson was promoting the intellectual views of popular eighteenth-century moral philosophers, particularly Jean Jacques Rousseau; who advocated that the first occupants of a territory rightfully owned the land.[42]

The paradox of Jefferson's support of overtly monopolistic principles within the treaty parallels the seemingly irrational ability of the Virginian to espouse tenets of democratic freedom, while simultaneously owning a substantial number of slaves. One could even advocate that Jefferson saw the treaty as a political

---

[40] Ibid.

[41] Ibid.

[42] Thomas John Kennedy, "The Origins of Creek Indian Nationalism: Contact, Diplomacy, Clans, and Intermarriage During the Colonial and Early National Periods," (M. A. Thes., University of Houston, 1992), 127; Gordon I. Bennett, "Aboriginal Title in the Common Law: A Stony Path Through Feudal Doctrine," Buffalo Law Review

compromise that could be used in order to advance some other unannounced political agenda in the future.[43] It is unknown as to whether Jefferson actually believed in the sovereignty of the Creek Confederacy, or was simply trying to convince Congress to support Washington's secret articles. Jefferson's activities were the reflection of pragmatic political attitude that, at its foundation, realized that ideological sacrifices were sometimes necessary in order to achieve an end result.

In regards to trade within the Confederacy, the 1790 Treaty of New York provided McGillivray with a near identical twin to the 1784 Treaty of Pensacola. Both treaties acknowledged some degree of Creek independence, provided protection of Creek territory, as well as guaranteed trade and access to European goods. In addition, McGillivray once again would legally control most, if not all, of the trade within the Confederacy; and was commissioned as a high-ranking military officer with pay. The Treaty of New York was advantageous for the Creek Confederacy, and did not conflict with the previous agreement with Spain. For the Creeks, the Treaty of New York provided addition insurance against aggressive Georgian border policies, and guaranteed the presence of emergency trade routes if Spanish channels were no longer available. With the signing of the Treaty of New York which recognized "all parts of the Creek Nation within the limits of the United States . . . to be under the protection of the United States of America," Alexander McGillivray had provided the Confederacy some measure of military and economic stability.[44]

---

27 (Fall 1978): 619.

43 Julian Boyd, a Jefferson historian and biographer, notes that, "the object [] was not only to legitimatize a monopoly but to accomplish this by treaty when it could not be done by statute." Boyd, The Papers of Thomas Jefferson vol. 17, 289; For a fuller understanding of early American political compromising see, Edmund S. Morgan, "Slavery and Freedom: The American Paradox," Journal of American History 59 (June 1972): 5-29.

44 Treaty with the Creeks, 1790, article II, Charles J. Kappler ed. Indian Treaties, 1778-1883 (New York: Interland Publishing

A political tactic for Native Americans during the eighteenth century was to align themselves with powerful European monarchies. Tribes that failed to do this were often destroyed or assimilated into neighboring tribal societies. Wise tribal leaders could even find success by playing rival European powers against each other, with McGillivray actions in 1790 fitting this political pattern. As was the case with the 1784, Treaty of Pensacola, a large military and economic power was legally obligated to protect the border rights of the Creek Confederacy. An important point is that the Treaty of New York clearly stipulated that the "Creek Nation will not hold any treaty with an individual State, or with individuals of any State."[45] A superficial glance at this stipulation implies a diminishment of Creek Indian freedoms and a severe restriction of the Confederacy's sovereignty. However, the provision, which allowed only for negotiations with the United States Federal government, actually provided valuable insurance against attacks from the state of Georgia.

The central source of trouble for the Creek Confederacy during the 1780s resulted from three legally dubious treaties with Georgia, which had been extracted from only a few Creek leaders. The Treaty of New York prevented any future Georgian attempts to promote treaties by restricting the power to negotiate to the United States' Federal government. Individual states could no longer claim a legal right to deal with McGillivray and the Confederacy, regardless of the circumstances.[46] The Creeks were even given the right to confront any invading Americans who were illegally occupying land (squatting) on the Confederacy's territory. Any non-

---

Inc., 1975), 25; Michael D. Green, "Alexander McGillivray," In Studies in Diversity: American Indian Leaders, ed. R. David Edmunds, 54-55.

[45] *Treaty of New York*, article II, Kappler Indian Treaties, 1778-1883, 25.

[46] Michael D. Green, "Alexander McGillivray," In Studies in Diversity: American Indian Leaders, ed. R. David Edmunds, 55.

Indian "shall forfeit the protection of the United States, and the Creeks may punish him or not, as they please."[47]

The United States' protection of the Creek Confederacy was a diplomatic triumph for McGillivray. The Creek Indians, for as long as they continued a defensive policy of resisting Georgia's invasions, legally bound the United States to defend Confederacy territory from encroachments. McGillivray had neutralized Georgia's ability to pursue a policy of aggressive frontier expansion. The Georgian officials had hoped to create a border crisis that would have forced the U. S. Federal government to provide military support to the state. The Treaty of New York, however, made the financial and military rescuing of the Georgians, at the expense of the Creek Confederacy, no longer an available option. The treaty provided McGillivray with a level of diplomatic flexibility, and due to the volatile nature of the regions politics, the treaty's clandestine provisions with the United States were kept secret from both the Georgians and Spanish officials.[48]

The Treaty of New York added another feature to McGillivray's multifaceted past. The principles used and enacted during the treaty negotiations were consistent with his earlier dealings with the British and the Spanish. One of the treaty's secret articles had granted McGillivray a full brigadier generalship within the United States army. Understandably, the granting of military rank and pay was the fledging United States' best parallel to McGillivray's Spanish commission.[49]

---

[47] *Treaty of New York*, article VI, Kappler, Indian Treaties, 1778-1883, 27.

[48] Michael D. Green, "Alexander McGillivray," In Studies in Diversity: American Indian Leaders, ed. R. David Edmunds, 56-57; Arthur Preston Whitaker, "Alexander McGillivray, 1789-1793," North Carolina Historical Review 5 (July 1928): 296-301.

[49] J. Leitch Wright Jr., "Creek-American Treaty of 1790: Alexander McGillivray and the Diplomacy of the Old Southwest," Georgia Historical Quarterly 21 (December 1967): 385-390.

The influential Indian leader, and former British officer, had now obtained the position of a paid American brigadier general, while concurrently maintaining the role of Spanish commissionary for the Creek Confederacy. What seemed as a conflict of interest was simply the unfolding of a complex web of social, political and economic relationships. McGillivray's Creek and Scottish ancestry, as well as experiences in the multi-ethnic Creek Nation, taught him ways to adapt and incorporate seemingly opposing cultural practices and ideals. These factors as independent elements appeared to contradict each other, yet when fused together, formed a complete and working whole. McGillivray had become a master at adapting and utilizing seemingly conflicting interests.

However, even McGillivray's diplomatic finesse possessed limits, with the Treaty of New York carrying a heavy price for the Creek Confederacy. The treaty forced the Indians to surrender about two-thirds of the disputed lands from the three previous 1780s treaties that had been made with Georgia. The relinquished tract of land was a three-million-acre strip located on the Confederacy's eastern border between the Ogeechee and Oconee Rivers. McGillivray had managed to hold on to a large piece of land immediately to the south of this three million acre strip, which included the prosperous hunting grounds of the Okefenokee Swamp. In exchange, the Confederacy received from the United States government an unspecified amount of goods as well as a perpetual annuity of fifteen hundred dollars for the land cession. However, some members of the Confederacy felt that the economic and political guarantees that McGillivray had gained were far too costly for the overall Creek Nation.[50]

.   .   .   .

---

[50] Ibid, 56; *Treaty of New York*, article IV, XII Kappler, Indian Treaties, 1778-1883, 26-28.

Documents depicting McGillivray's travel to New York in the summer of 1790 vividly describe the Creek's *Great Beloved Man* in detail. His American travelling companion, Colonel Marinus Willett, presented an account of the Native American leader which does not fit the racist stereotype of a savage, half-breed Indian. "After delivering him my introductory letter, I had some conversation with him; and after a good supper, and most kind entertainment, I went to bed, happy in being under the same roof with the man I have traveled thus far to see. Colonel M[c]'Gillivray appears to be a man of an open, candid, generous mind, with a good judgment, and a very tenacious memory."[51]

Another account of McGillivray from this time period is offered, interestingly enough, in a letter between Abigail Adams and her sister-in-law, Mary Cranch. In August of 1790, John and Abigail Adams had entertained McGillivray and the other members of his entourage during their stay in New York City. Abigail's correspondence implies that she was equally entertained by the Creek party's presence. "These are the first savages I ever saw. Mico Maco, one of their kings dined here yesterday and after dinner he confered a Name upon me, the meaning of which I do not know: Mammea." Abigail enthusiastically continued by stating that, "They are very fine looking Men, [with] placid countenances & fine shape."[52] Her account of McGillivray, like Willett's, conflicts with some of the stereotypical historical views of McGillivray as a "neurotic half-breed."[53] "MacGillivray dresses in our fashion speaks English like a Native & I should never suspect him to be of

---

[51] Willett, <u>Military Actions of Colonel Marinus Willett</u>, 101.

[52] Stewart Mitchell ed., <u>New Letters of Abigail Adams, 1788-1801</u> (Westport, Connecticut: Greenwood Press, Publishers, 1947), 56.

[53] Arthur Preston Whitaker, "Alexander McGillivray, 1783-1789," <u>North Carolina Historical Review</u> 5 (April 1928): 202-203.

that Nation, as he is not very dark.   He is grave and solid, intelligent and much of a Gentleman, but in very bad Health."[54]

Colonel Marinus Willett's and Abigail Adams' accounts of McGillivray display an individual that does not fit the Georgians' view who, "Long after his death, . . . continued to curse his memory."[55] The Creek leader's diverse cultural background created a historical identity that also baffled some earlier historians, who saw McGillivray's abilities as "a bizarre confusion of sophistication and primitive illogicality."[56]   In fact, some of these same scholars described the Indian leader's personality as a mixture of volatile components that created "the most felicitous compound of kind ever seen."[57]

These conflicting accounts of McGillivray's character, as well as his flexible view of diplomacy and economics, could create the impression of an individual who is devoid of any moral or ethical principles.   On the contrary, he possessed strong personal loyalties to the Creek Confederacy, his trading partner William Panton, as well as a sense of personal ethics.   The specific military and political actions performed during his life demonstrated an individual who was anything but a simple opportunist.

McGillivray realized that his dual-cultural identity, Creek and Scottish, had provided him with an invaluable education; which was an opportunity that he attempted to pass on to future generations within the Creek Confederacy.   One of the secret articles from the Treaty of New York stated that, "the United States agree[s] to educate and clothe such of the Creek youth as shall be agreed upon, not exceeding four in number at any one

---

[54] Mitchell ed., New letters of Abigail Adams,   57.
[55] Whitaker,   "Alexander McGillivray, 1783-1789,"   181.
[56] Ibid; Absalom H. Chappell,   Miscellanies of Georgia, Historical, Biographical, Descriptive, Etc.   (Atlanta, Georgia: James F. Meegan,   1874),   28.
[57] Ibid.

time."[58]   The Creek-Scot Indian leader was well aware that a classic education would greatly aid future Creek Indian generations in regards to the fields of international diplomacy and trade.

McGillivray's life had taught him that these cross-cultural connections, that often develop due to education; were crucial for providing the "tools" that successful allowed societies to adapt and overcome challenging political and economic environments. In the spirit of this concept, while in New York during the treaty negotiations, McGillivray left his own nephew under the protection and tutelage of the U. S. Secretary of War, Henry Knox.   The Spanish agent reported this fact back to his commanders stating that, "I inquired of McGuillibray [sic] as to his [Alexander's nephew] whereabouts. He replied that Minister Knox had taken him under his charge in order to give him a cultivated education."[59]

When McGillivray was questioned by the Spanish about leaving his nephew in the care of American hands, his reported reply was "that with pleasure he would give over another nephew to be brought up as a Spaniard."[60] The Indian leader's actions do not display the short-sighted rationale of a greedy opportunist, or a well-positioned cultural *broker* who cheated on all involved parties in order to gain a profit. His policy of sending Creek Indian youths to learn of the outside world demonstrates the actions of a leader who was genuinely concerned with the future of his political state.

By chance or design, McGillivray's actions in this instance possess a parallel to the cultural traditions of Scottish clans, which practiced the custom of "fosterage" in order to more fully bind large clans together.   Fosterage in Scotland's clan society usually consisted of the exchanging of infant members or one family raising

---

[58] *Treaty of New York, Secret Articles*, Article V, De Pauw, Senate Executive Journal and Related Documents, 249.
[59] *Carlos Howard* to *Quesada*, September 24, 1790, Caughey, McGillivray of the Creeks, 283.
[60] Ibid.

another family's children.   The custom was so thoroughly integrated into Scottish Highland society that even the sons of the clan chiefs were included in the practice.   The purpose of the exchange was to allow one half of the clan society to know how the other half lived, ultimately creating a more unified clan system. The motivation behind the practice is reflected in an ancient Gaelic proverb, "affectionate to a man is a friend, but a foster-brother is as the life of his heart."[61] There is no evidence which explicitly states that McGillivray was consciously adhering to Scottish Clan customs when this provision was added to the Treaty of New York, but the cultural parallel does exist.

Another act that displays a deeper view of McGillivray's moral character and internal workings took place in Pensacola during the American Revolution. McGillivray created a "Parole of Honor" that permitted nine Spanish prisoners to go free, on the condition that the Spaniards would pledge to release nine British prisoners once they reached New Orleans. The parole's wording stated that the Spanish prisoners "will remain, and consider ourselves as prisoners of War, to return to any of the British Dominions if called upon, unless Exchanged for the men [British prisoners] under mentioned," displays a profound sense of sagacity and trust.[62] McGillivray was not a saint, but he did possess a moral foundation and a sense of justice. His creation of this "Parole of Honor" displays the presence of an internal code of honor, ethics, and proper conduct.

During his journey to New York in 1790, additional valuable insights into McGillivray's personal character were

---

[61] Robert Bain, Clans and Tartans of Scotland Margaret O MacDougall ed. (London and Glasgow: Collins, 1968), 17.

[62] John Walton Caughey, Bernardo de Galvez in Louisiana, 1776-1783 (Gretna: Pelican Publishing Company, 1972), 232. For a full description of the war activities which lead to the "Parole of Honor" refer to, Caughey, Bernardo de Galvez in Louisiana, 187-214.

recorded by observers. In North Carolina, at the Guilford court house, McGillivray was greeted by a Mrs. Brown who had been a former prisoner of the Creek Confederacy. A party of Indians had killed her husband and taken her, as well as their children, captive. McGillivray had redeemed Mrs. Brown from captivity and allowed her to live on his plantation for a year before she eventually returned to the United States. The documentation of the occurrence does not state the fate of Mrs. Brown's children, or why she stayed for a full year at McGillivray's home within the Creek Confederacy. Their meeting at the court house in Guilford was curtly summed up as "truly affecting."[63] Some historians have argued that the Creek leader paid a ransom for all of the remaining survivors of Brown family and graciously provided for them afterwards. Regardless of the exact details surrounding Mrs. Brown stay within the Creek Confederacy, McGillivray's actions do not display the traits of a petty tyrant.[64]

· · · ·

The *patron-client* relationship between Spain and McGillivray had become strained by the late 1780s. Acts of American aggression on the eastern borders of the Creek Confederacy had created a cooling effect between the Creek leader (*broker*) and his Spanish allies (*patron*). Spain did not desire a direct military confrontation with the United States. In this sense, the Creek Confederacy was only a military buffer and ally, not actual Spanish controlled territory.

---

[63] Willett, A Narrative of the Military Actions of Colonel Marinus Willett, 111.

[64] Carolyn Thomas Foreman, "Alexander McGillivray, Emperor of the Creeks," Chronicles of Oklahoma 7 (March 1929): 114; Albert James Pickett, "McGillivray of the Creeks," Alabama Historical Quarterly (Summer 1930): 134; Richard Lewis Campbell, Historical Sketches of Colonial Florida (Cleveland: Williams Publishing Company, 1892; reprint, Gainesville: The University Presses of Florida, 1975), 185-186.

Spain's reluctance to support the Confederacy had forced McGillivray to search for a new *patron*, which ultimately lead to peace overtures with the United States federal government. Nearly all surviving accounts detailing McGillivray's 1790 treaty with the United States display the Creek leader's dynamic and flexible worldview. The Creek leader was always in search of diplomatic or economic ways that would guarantee the Confederacy's territorial borders.

The Treaty of New York in 1790 carried profound implications for both the Creek Confederacy and the United States. The United States, under the leadership of George Washington, had created a legal precedent by directly negotiating with McGillivray. The treaty allowed the Creek Indian leader many of same privileges afforded under the earlier 1784 Treaty of Pensacola. McGillivray's adherence to two separate treaties, from opposing national powers, demonstrates a complex and pragmatic view of diplomacy, economics, and politics.

Alexander McGillivray is unique when compared to many other American Indian resistance leaders of the eighteenth and nineteenth centuries. Divinely inspired aspirations, visions, or religious dogma were never part of his search for tangible solutions to the Creek Confederacy's problems. He did not pursue a policy of perceived past Native American culture purity that often advocated a rejection of all things non-Indian such as European religions, trade items, and technology. Later Indian leaders from Tecumseh to Sitting Bull would take part in mass revitalization movements, which were heavily based on mysticism and the preservation of Native American culture. However, for McGillivray these were not realistic solutions.

Instead, he firmly and gravely focused his efforts on the present, with the hope of creating a survivable future for the Creek people and their nation. The remedies he presented for Creek

Indian survival had been learned from a variety sources and influences, ranging from Creek, Scot, British, Spanish, and American. McGillivray's ability to create a *coalescence* of various cultural, social, and political factors was fully personified towards the end of his life.

The term *coalescence* is not regularly used in the context of social or political history. However, it is the most suitable term to use when examining the life of Alexander McGillivray. Coalescence is usually defined as the combining of diverse items or features. It is seen as a process of separate "entities" merging together to form one new "entity". This process of merging or assimilating different customs and ideas is plainly evident in McGillivray's life. His profound understanding of the political and social landscape of the late-eighteenth century southeastern region, provided the Creek Confederacy with its best opportunity to maintain its territorial sovereignty.

Chapter 6

♦

The Life of Alexander McGillivray, 1750 - 1793

Throughout McGillivray's life there were crucial periods that allowed for the development of essential leadership skills. These abilities later became a great asset for the Creek Confederacy and its struggle to defend their way of life, if not their very existence, in the Southern backcountry. Hints from McGillivray's early life provide coincidental evidence of cultural parallels perhaps existing between traditional Scottish Highland immigrants and the indigenous Creek Indians. McGillivray's Scottish-Creek ancestry provided him with a rich, but complicated, cultural heritage; which allowed him to establish kinship networks that eventually expanded into economic and political opportunities. His ability to exploit these opportunities became a key factor during his early adulthood. Talent, luck, and family connections within Creek and colonial European culture allowed McGillivray to become an interpreter for the British during the Revolutionary War.

The closing of the American Revolution found Alexander McGillivray in an advantageous position as one of the preeminent Indian leaders within the Creek Confederacy, who had gained valuable experience as a commissioned British officer. After the Revolution, his military position assisted him in gaining access to existing trade networks within the Confederacy, as well as connecting to surviving pro-loyalist interest within southern colonial society. Eventually, McGillivray capitalized upon these previously developed Scottish and Creek trade connections, greatly increasing his overall political and economic influence within the Southeast. His mother's kinship networks, as well as his father's Scottish business connections, became even more entrenched after the development of a *patron-client* relationship with Spain. Former Scottish business contacts solidified and were maintained through Spanish military and economic support. McGillivray's clientage relationship with Spain becomes another crucial piece in his evolution as a political leader.

McGillivray's political and economic development continued as a *client* of the Spanish Crown, which allowed him to become an increasingly influential Creek leader. Spanish supplies, as well as access to British trade goods obtained through Spanish ports, allowed the Creeks by the mid-1780s to neutralize Georgian military threats on the Confederacy's eastern border. However, the conflict between the state of Georgia and the Creek Confederacy started to concern the newly appointed leaders of the United States federal government.

Towards the end of McGillivray's life he was able to develop a political relationship with the recently formed United States of America, while simultaneously preserving previous established diplomatic and economic connections. Even as he maintained his positions as a Spanish officer, a Creek Indian leader, and a successful merchant; he was also appointed a United States Brigadier General. By 1791, McGillivray had become the link or cultural nexus in a highly developed and complex maze of economic relationships, kinship networks, and political alliances.

In the fields of politics, diplomacy, and trade; McGillivray was a master at using his cultural connections to benefit the overall welfare of the Creek Confederacy. His sophisticated understanding of the political and cultural landscape of the late eighteenth-century southeastern region allowed him to gain access to different spheres of influence. Various family kinship connections, knowledge of languages, as well as a familiarity with colonial (Scottish) social practices; created what was essentially a cultural *broker* or *mediator*.

Individuals who became *brokers* are usually able to cross existing cultural barriers while sometimes profiting in the process. McGillivray's diplomatic successes suggest an evolution from a cultural intermediary or interpreter position, into the position of a cultural *broker*. McGillivray maintained a *broker* position while concurrently assuming the role of a *client* under the Spanish government's patronage. Spain's *patron-client* relationship, however, soon became too restrictive for McGillivray's needs. The Creek leader was forced to expand his diplomatic influence in order to maintain the Creek Confederacy's autonomy in an increasingly hostile political environment. The final evolutionary stage of McGillivray's life is best defined as the synchronization of many social variables, personal traits, and political connections into a definable social-economic position. For McGillivray, this cultural position and overall identity always possessed a pro-Creek orientation. This constantly shifting and adapting of influence and control is best described as a process of *cultural coalescence*.

Over the span of McGillivray's life, a linear progression of influential connections is evident. However, his culturally diverse background and variety of political and economic positions has baffled some historians. One early scholar described him as "heir to [sic] two natures, which co-existed in him seemingly without conflict and with great force and harmony of development."[1] McGillivray's rich cultural heritage did not create a scheming, Machiavellian-style, uncaring political leader; who simply became a

---

[1] Absalom H. Chappell, <u>Miscellanies of Georgia, Historical, Biographical, Descriptive, Etc.</u> (Atlanta: James F. Meegan, 1874), 28.

superb opportunist. His personal identity was that of a Creek Indian and he worked tirelessly to promote the Confederacy's welfare, which were intricately connected to his own personal interests.

President George Washington's comment that, "Mr. McGillivray is stated to possess great abilities" fails to adequately describe the leadership qualities of the Creek Indian leader.[2] McGillivray was a perplexing historical figure who possessed a complex cultural heritage, but was always loyal to his Native American identity. He had attempted to hold back the increasingly aggressive tide of American settlers by advocating that the Creek Confederacy was a sovereign nation state with legitimate border rights. His feeling of hostility towards the arrogance of the Americans was evident in his personal letters. "Intoxicated with high Ideas of National Consequence from having unexpectedly gain[e]d the establishment of their Independency, they Vainly Imagined themselves what they affected to Style themselves, Conquerors of the old & Masters of the New World." The same note also portrays McGillivray's ire towards the Americans' western Indian policy, "In this dream of greatness & Power they fondly thought that they cou[l]d Seize with Impunity every foot of Territory belonging to the Red Natives of America."[3]

These statements readily displayed McGillivray's pro-Native American identity, yet there was a unique distinctiveness to his personality. He is easily defined as an American Indian resistance leader in the same tradition as other late-eighteenth and early-nineteenth-century individuals. Leaders like Chief Pontiac of

---

[2] Instructions to the Commissioners for Southern Indians [from George Washington], August 29, 1789, Linda Grant De Pauw ed., Senate Executive Journal and Related Documents (Baltimore: John Hopkins University Press, 1974), 205.

[3] *McGillivray of Miro*, August 10, 1789, John Walton Caughey, McGillivray of the Creeks, (Norman: University of Oklahoma, 1959), 244.

the Ottawa or Tecumseh of the Shawnee share with McGillivray an unyielding desire to defend the integrity of their existing tribal borders through the use of a pan-Indian resistance.[4] However, the Creek Indian leader's dualistic cultural ancestry provided another dimension in his overall ability to adapt and survive new political and economic situations. The mystical or religious motivations of Tecumseh and his brother the Prophet or later leaders like Sitting Bull, which advocated a return to pre-contact tribal customs and practices; were never voiced in McGillivray's letters or speeches.

As an industrious leader and merchant with European ancestry, McGillivray did not voice a political view that wished to expel all European influences from Native American societies. Merely rejecting all things European was not realistically possible for the Creek leader or the Confederacy. His personal ancestry included Scottish traditions, and he enjoyed many of the conveniences and technological wonders that European colonial society offered. His familiarity with British society is displayed by the fact that he was fully fluent in the English language. Eyewitness accounts of the leader noted that he was able to use elegant English "in Haste, and in a Circle of many Chieftains, whose Garrulity would have confused any other Man than M'Gillivray."[5] McGillivray's solutions for Indian survival were far more progressive. The overriding goal of Creek Indian autonomy and survival was paramount, regardless of whether the solution arose from European or Native American influences.

McGillivray's intellectual flexibility allowed him to consider multiple political solutions. He possessed an ability to

---

[4] Gregory E. Dowd, "Thinking and Believing: Nativism and Unity in the Ages of Pontiac and Tecumseh," American Indian Quarterly 16 (Summer 1992): 309-311, 329.

[5] John Pope, A Tour Through The Southern and Western Territories of the United States of United States of North - America, (Richmond: John Dixion, 1792; reprint, Gainesville: University of Florida Press, 1979) 51-52.

perceive the world with a holistic understanding which allowed him to perceive numerous available options. This broader worldview was often created due to the varied experiences of individuals who possess a multi-cultural ancestry. This fact perhaps explains why in many Native American societies during the eighteenth and nineteenth centuries, it was "mixed" ancestry individuals, or American mestizos, who usually created or introduced new inventions or improvements to their Indian societies. Many of these improvements were made to pre-existing Native American tools and weaponry, but these changes were also made to political and social institutions.[6] McGillivray, like many other Native American leaders who were ethnically Indian and European, possessed an uncanny ability to creatively solve problems. However, these "abilities" extended far beyond the modification of muskets or farm implements. He transformed Creek Indian political and economic institutions with elements of European traditions and culture, with the goal of finding the best solutions for the Confederacy's survival.

McGillivray altered and used European diplomatic ideals and tools in order to fit the Creek Confederacy's political circumstances, while simultaneously maintaining a Native American cultural identity.[7] Any acceptance of a foreign cultural trait is likely adapted in a way that effectively harmonizes the alien characteristic into the adopting group's own traditions. During times of stress, if a besieged culture can understand and assimilate a foreign, and often threatening, society's influences, then these foreign ideas can serve as effective guides for future actions.

---

[6] Dean R. Snow, The Iroquois (Oxford and Cambridge: Blackwell Publishers, 1994) 120.

[7] Carol R. Ember & Melvin Ember, Cultural Anthropology (Englewood Cliffs, New Jersey: Prentice Hall, 1990), 320-321; Anthony F. C. Wallace, Religion: An Anthropological View (New York: Random House, 1966), 30; Cronon, William, Changes in the Land: Indians, Colonists, and the Ecology of New England (New York:

However, these European influences, as well as the Creek-Scot leader's exposure and receptiveness to them, only partially explain his life. McGillivray's historical circumstances provide insight into the nature of his character, with his persona displaying the experiences of a person who, like an actor; played many different roles. His various life experiences show evidence of an individual who, over the course of his life, assumed many social and political roles. Roles that at an initial glance appear to conflict with each other, yet in reality were a linear progression of growth and adaptation.

This means that the individual, who became a commissioned British officer during the American Revolution and assumed the role of an interpreter; was different from the person who had created an alliance with Spain and the Creek Confederacy in 1784. These earlier roles fail to fully encompass the triangular-shaped economic relationship between McGillivray, the Panton's company, and Spain. Nor do they capture the shrewdness of his economic and diplomatic maneuverings with the state of Georgia, and later, the United States of America.

Historians and anthropologists have pointed out that certain cultural roles possess a fluid-like quality, in which a *broker* is able to assume a *patron's* role, while a *patron* can move into a *brokerage* position.[8] McGillivray, however, appeared to possess the ability to occupy various cultural positions simultaneously, and instead of becoming marginalized in these activities; assumed a "culturally enlarged" position.[9] This "enlarged" position was a direct result of McGillivray's evolutionary process from *interpreter* to *broker*, and then from a *broker* to both a *patron* as well as a

Hill and Wang, 1983), 163-164.

[8] Margaret Connell Szasz, Between Indian and White Worlds (Norman: University of Oklahoma Press, 1994), 12.

[9] Ibid, 19; James Clifton ed., Being and Becoming Indian: Biographical Studies of North American Frontiers (Chicago: Dorsey

client. This evolution in his social position eventually redefined his political and economic position in the Southeastern region.

McGillivray's past connections, relationships, and skills unfolded into a broad web of connections. Each strand of this web connected to a variety of sources, from Scot and Creek, to Spanish and American – all of which were directly tied to McGillivray. From 1790 to 1793, his leadership position became a cultural nexus, with this stage of his life allowing him to evolve from a *patron/client* relationship into an all-encompassing role best described as a cultural *coalescence*.

Epilogue

♦

The Creek Confederacy After McGillivray

McGillivray was by far one of the most influential Creek leaders from the Revolutionary and Federalist time period. At the peak of his political career he was able secure both trade and territorial guarantees from both Spain and the United States, while simultaneously maintaining access to pre-Revolution British trade networks. The Creek Confederacy possessed a stable, but temporary political and economic arrangement by the time of Alexander McGillivray's death on February 17, 1793. However, the Creek's territorial stability would drastically change after his death.

Even after signing the Treaty of New York in 1790, many Americans officials still hungered for Creek territory. Out of a fear that the United States government would renege on its treaty obligations, McGillivray negotiated an additional treaty with Spain in 1792. Until his death, the Creek leader would continue to meet with Spanish, British, and American officials; always seeking the best diplomatic solution for the Creek Confederacy. Unfortunately, the following decades were not kind to the Native Americans of the Southern backcountry.

By November 1794, the United States signed Jay's Treaty with Great Britain, settling many of the backcountry issues that had been left unresolved from the American Revolution. In less than a year, by October 1795, the United States had also signed

Pinckney's Treaty which established friendly relations between the United States and Spain. McGillivray's diplomatic policy of seeking a political balance between Spanish and American interest, in order to achieve a sense of territorial stability for the Creek Indians; had disintegrated.

Both Jay's and Pinckney's treaties formalized relations between the United States, Great Britain, and Spain. These treaties established the territorial sovereignty of the United States over the region to the west of Appalachian Mountains. America's borders not only extended from the Atlantic seaboard to the Mississippi River, but were officially recognized by the two most powerful political influences in the region -- Great Britain and Spain.

During the next decades, two of McGillivray's nephews, William Weatherford and William McIntosh, would also rise to political prominence within the Creek Confederacy. However, by the end of the Creek War in 1814, the Creek Indians were forced to surrender over 23 million acres of territory to the United States. The passing of the Indian Removal Act in 1830 by the U. S. Congress eliminated most, if not all, of the political influence that the Creek Confederacy still possessed in the southeastern region. By the end of the 1830s, most of the Five Civilized Tribes (Cherokee, Chickasaw, Choctaw, Creek and Seminole) had been forcibly moved to lands west of the Mississippi River.

The term Manifest Destiny was not coined until the 1840s, but the movement of colonist, Europeans, and slaves to the west had occurred since the earliest days of the Jamestown and Plymouth colonies. Alexander was one in long line of Native American leaders who attempted to resist the constant territory pressure from both European colonists and American settlers. For a brief period, the Creek Confederacy was able to enjoy some degree of political and economic equilibrium, largely due to the leadership of McGillivray. During the last years of his life, using a mixture of political finesse and economic connections; the advancement of the Americans was halted. His diverse experiences provided the Creek Confederacy with a more flexible and dynamic responses, which ultimately provided greater success and survival in a world that was rapidly changing for both Alexander and the Creek Confederacy.

18th Century Southeastern Native American Settlements*

Upper and Lower Creek Nation (45 total)

Coosa Old Town	Weetomkee	Little Coweta
Tallassehasee	Little Oakchoys	Great Coweta
Abicouchi	Mukalasses	Natchi
Coweta New Town	Savannah	Clayatskee
Mulberry tree	White Ground	Cussita
Waccokay	Coolamie	Woristo
Hittabie	Cloonellas	Ocmulgie
Ruknatallahassa	James Germany	Hitcheta
Weeoka	Ottassy	Palachocota
Oakfuskee	Oallobe	Occonee
Cailedgie	Wallhal	Swagala
Little Tallassie	Atchasapa	Swagalatchie
Hickary Ground	Tickabale	Lower Eufalla
Oakchoys	Great Tassie	Tuassie
Coosada	Chawelatchie	Halfway

Choctaw Nation (58 total)

Chikilk Batcha	Enany	Iyukkene
West Imongoolasha	Okahoola	Coosa
Conchapa Consapa	Sypeessa	Olitassa
Abitapoocolochitto	Aithee Uckehuca	Bishasha
Chomontakai	Osuktalaya	Chanke
Oaka Loosa	Tonicahaw	Oka Copassa
Slank Aullah	West Obeika	Oony
East Yasoo	West Yasoo	Coastraw
Cabeahoola	Tallow	Panthe
Aithee Aimithaw	West Congetto	Oskelagna
Bobue Toocolochitto	Kaffittalaya	Bishcoon
Oka Attackla	Senekahaw	Senekchaw
Escoola	Oka Ooopely	Olaskshanabe
East Congeeto	Alleon Loanshaw	Ashookawaya
Lushasha	Shanhaw	Ayanabe
Imongolacha Skalani	Okapoola	Talpahoka
Ebitapoocolo Skalani	Oka Chippo	Chicasawhay
Conchatiekpe	Yagne Shoogama	Sooctoloose
Choocahoola	Custachas	East Abuka

Chickasaw Nation (11 total)

Chicalaia Opays Matahaw T.	Hickihaw	Chukasalaya
Rubby's Hog Craul	Mellataw	Ashuck Hooma
Opay Mattahaw's Plantation	Tuckewillow	Chatclaw
Commissary McIntosh's Plantation		
McGillwray and Strather's Plantation		

Cherokee Nation was divided into three general groups (79 total)

#1 - Over the Hills and Valley Settlements (43 total)
#2 - Middle Settlements (25 total)
#3 - Lower Settlements (11 total)

*From part of the parcel map Compiled around 1770 concerning British Indian Trade, in Swanton, John R., Early History of the Creek Indians and Their Neighbors (Government Printing Office: Washington), 1922, Map attached to inside of back cover.

Bibliography

◆

Primary Sources

Adair, James. The History of the American Indians. (Edward and Charles Dilly: London), 1775.

Bartram, William. Travels through North & South Carolina, Georgia, East & West Florida, The Cherokee Country, The Extensive Territories of the Muscogulges, or Creek Confederacy, and the country of the Chactaws. (R.R. Donnelly & Sons Company: Harrisonburg, Virginia), 1988.

Boyd, Julian P. ed. The Papers of Thomas Jefferson. vol. 17 (Princeton University Press: Princeton, New Jersey), 1965.

Caughey, John Walton. McGillivray of the Creeks. (University of Oklahoma Press: Norman), 1959.

Caughey, John Walton. Bernado de Galvez in Louisiana, 1776 – 1783. (Gretna: Pelican Publishing Company), 1972.

Corbitt, Duvon C., ed. and tr. "Papers Relating to the Georgia – Florida Frontier, 1784-1800," Georgia Historical Quarterly 20 (December 1936): 356-358; 21 (March 1937): 73-83.

Coulter, E. Merton and Saye, Albert B. ed. A List of the Early Settlers of Georgia. (Athens, Georgia: University of Georgia Press), 1949.

Crevecoeur, J. Hector St. John. Letters from An American Farmer. London: Thomas Davis, 1782; reprint, Gloucester, Massachusetts: Peter Smith, 1968.

Davis, Robert S. Jr. Georgia Citizens and Soldiers of the American Revolution. (Southern Historical Press Inc: Easley, South Carolina), 1979.

DePauw, Linda Grant ed. Senate Executive Journal and Related
     Documents. (Johns Hopkins University Press: Baltimore),
     1974.

Fitzpatrick, John C. ed. The Writings of George Washington: from
     the Original Manuscript Sources, 1745 – 1799. vol. 30, 31,
     32, & 38 (United States Printing Office: Washington),
     1939 - 1944.

Hawkins, Benjamin. A Sketch of the Creek Country. Georgia
     Historical Society Collections Vol. III, (Kraus Reprint
     Company: New York), 1971.

Kappler, Charles J. Indian Treaties, 1778-1883. (New York:
     Interland Publishing Inc.), 1975.

Lawson, John. A New Voyage to Carolina. London, 1709; reprint,
     Ann Arbor University Microfilms, Inc: 1966.

McDowell, William L. Jr. ed. Colonial Records of South Carolina:
     Documents relating to Indian Affairs, May 21, 1750 –
     August 7, 1754. Columbia: South Carolina Archives
     Department, 1958.

McGillivray, Lachlan. *Last will and testament.* June 12, 1767,
     Montgomery, Alabama: Alabama Department of Archives
     and History.

McPherson, Robert G. ed. The Journal of the Earl of Egmont:
     Abstract of the Trustees Proceedings for Establishing the
     Colony of Georgia, 1732 – 1738. (Athens: University of
     Georgia Press), 1962.

Milfort, General Louis. Memoire ou coup d' oel rapide sur mes
     differens voyages et mon sejour dans la nation Creck.
     McCary, Ben C. ed. And tr., [Memoirs of a quick glance at
     my various travels and my sojourn in the Creek Nation].
     Paris, 1802; reprint, Kennesaw, Georgia: Continental
     Book Company, 1959.

Mitchell, Stewart ed. New Letters of Abigail Adams, 1788 – 1801.
     (Greenwood Press, Publishers: Westport, Connecticut),
     1973.

Moore, Caroline T. ed. Abstracts of the Wills of the State of South
     Carolina, 1740 – 1760. (Columbia: R. L. Bryan), 1964.

Pope, John. <u>A Tour Through the Southern and Western Territories</u>
<u>of the United States of North – America</u>. Richmond,
Virginia: John Dixion, 1792; reprint, Gainesville:
University of Florida Press, 1979.

Romans, Bernard. <u>A Concise Natural History of East and west</u>
<u>Florida</u>. 1775; reprint, Gainesville: University of Florida
Press, 1962.

Swan, Major Caleb. <u>Position and State of Manners and Arts in the</u>
<u>Creek, or Muscogee Nation in 1791</u>. Philadelphia, 1795;
reprint in, Schoolcraft, Henry R., <u>Information Respecting</u>
<u>the History, Condition and Prospects of the Indian Tribes</u>
<u>of the United States</u>. vol. v, (Philadelphia: Lippincott,
Gambo), 1851-1857.

Syrett, Harold C. ed. and Cooke, Jacob E. ed. <u>The Papers of</u>
<u>Alexander Hamilton, December 1789 - August 1790</u>. vol. 6
(Columbia University Press: New York), 1962.

Bibliography

♦

Secondary Sources: Monographs

Axtell, James. Beyond 1492: Encounter in Colonial North America. (New York and Oxford: Oxford University Press), 1992.

_____. The European and the Indian: Essays in the Ethnohistory of Colonial North America. (New York and Oxford: Oxford University Press), 1981.

_____. The Invasion Within: The Contact of Cultures in Colonial North America. (New York and Oxford: Oxford University Press), 1985.

Bailyn, Bernard. The Peopling of British North America: An Introduction. (New York: Vintage Books), 1988.

Bain, Robert. Clans and Tartans of Scotland. MacDougall, Margaret O. ed., (London & Glasgow: Collins), 1968.

Berman, Harold J. Law and Revolution: The Formation of the Western Legal Tradition. (Cambridge: Harvard University Press), 1983.

Booker, Karen M. Languages of the Aboriginal Southeast. (Metuchen, New Jersey: Scarecrow Press, Inc), 1991.

Bowden, Henry Warner. American Indians and Christian Missions: Studies in Cultural Conflict. (Chicago: University of Chicago Press), 1981.

Bodley, John H. Cultural Anthropology: Tribes, States and the Global System. (Mountain View, California: Mayfield Publishing Company), 1994.

Calloway, James E. The Early Settlement of Georgia. (Athens, Georgia: University of Georgia Press), 1948.

Campbell, Richard L. Historical Sketches of Colonial Florida.
(Gainesville: The University Presses of Florida), 1975.

Cashin, Edward J. Lachlan McGillivray, Indian Trader: The
Shaping of the Southern Colonial Frontier. (Athens and
London: The University of Georgia Press), 1992.

Chapman, George. Chief William McIntosh: A Man of Two Worlds.
(Atlanta, Georgia: Cherokee Publishing Company) 1988.

Chiapelli, Fredi ed. First Images of America: The Impact of the
New World Upon the Old. vol. 2 (Berkeley: University of
California Press), 1976.

Coker, William S. and Watson, Thomas D. Indian Traders of the
Spanish Borderlands: Panton, Leslie & Company and
John Forbes & Company, 1783 – 1847. (Pensacola:
University of West Florida Press), 1986.

Coleman, Kenneth ed., A History of Georgia. (Athens, Georgia:
University of Georgia Press), 1977.

Corkran, David H. The Creek Frontier, 1540-1783. (Norman:
University of Oklahoma Press), 1967.

Clifton, James ed. Being and Becoming Indian: Biographical
Studies of North American Frontiers. (Chicago: Dorsey
Press), 1989.

Cronon, William. Changes in the Land: Indians, Colonists, and the
Ecology of the New England. (New York: Hill and Wang),
1983.

Daiches, David. A Companion to Scottish Culture. (Holmes &
Meier Publishers, Inc: New York), 1981.

Dunbar, John Telfar. History of Highland Dress. (Edinburgh,
Scotland: Oliver and Boyd), 1962.

Dockstader, Frederick J. Great North American Indians: Profiles
in Life and Leadership. (New York: Van Nostrand
Reinhold Company), 1977.

Dowd, Gregory Evans. A Spirited Resistance: The North American
Indian Struggle for Unity, 1745-1815. (Baltimore and
London : Johns Hopkins University Press), 1992.

Edmunds, R David ed. Studies in Diversity: American Indian Leaders. (Lincoln: University of Nebraska), 1989.

Ember, Carol R. & Ember, Melvin. Cultural Anthropology. 12edition (New Jersey: Prentice Hall, Inc), 2005.

Fagan, Brain M. Ancient North America: The Archaeology of a Continent. (New York: Thames and Hudson), 1991.

_____. Clash of Cultures. (New York: W.H. Freeman and Company), 1984.

Gillis, Michael J. ed. Essays in North American Indian History. (Dubuque, Iowa: Kendall/Hunt publishing Company), 1990.

Grant, I. F. and Cheape, Hugh. Periods in Highland History. (London: Shepheard - Walwyn limited), 1987.

Green, Michael D. The Creeks: A Critical Bibliography. (Bloomington and London: Indiana University Press), 1979.

_____. The Politics of Indian Removal: Creek Government and Society in Crisis. (Lincoln and London: University of Nebraska Press), 1982.

Griffith, Benjamin W. Jr. McIntosh and Weatherford, Creek Indian Leaders. (Tuscaloosa and London: University of Alabama Press), 1988.

Griffith, Lucille. Alabama: A Documentary History to 1900. (Tuscaloosa: University of Alabama Press), 1968.

Harviland, William A. Cultural Anthropology: The Human Challenge. 12 edition (New York: Wadsworth Publishing), 2007.

Hardin, Terri ed. Legends & Lore of the American Indians. (New York: Barnes & Noble, Inc), 1993.

Henri, Florette. The Southern Indians and Benjamin Hawkins: 1796-1816. (Norman and London: University of Oklahoma Press), 1986.

Houston, R. A. ed. and Whyte, I. D. ed. Scottish Society, 1500 – 1800. (Cambridge: Cambridge University Press), 1989.

Hudson, Charles M. ed. Four Centuries of Southern Indians. (Athens, Georgia: The University of Georgia Press), 1975.

Hurtado, Albert L. & Iverson, Peter ed. Major Problems in American Indian History: Documents and Essays. (Lexington, Massachusetts: Wadsworth Publishing), 2000.

Jennings, Francis. The Invasion of America: Indians, Colonialism and the Cant of Conquest. (Chapel Hill: University of North Carolina Press), 2010.

Jones, Dorothy V. Licence for Empire: Colonialism by Treaty in Early America. (Chicago: University of Chicago Press), 1982.

Jones, Grant D. and Kautz, Robert R. ed. The Transition to Statehood in the New World. (New York & Cambridge: Cambridge University Press), 1981.

Knollenberg, Bernhard. George Washington: The Virginia Period, 1732 - 1775. (Durham, North Carolina: Duke University Press), 1964.

Lynch, John. Spanish Colonial Administration, 1782 – 1810: The Intendant System in the Viceroyalty of Rio de la Plata. (London: Athlone Press University of London), 1958.

Mahon, John K. ed. Indians of the Lower South: Past and Present. (Pensacola: Gulf Coast History and Humanities Conference), 1975.

Martin, Calvin ed. The American Indian and the Problem of History. (Oxford: Oxford University Press), 1987.

Martin, Joel W. Sacred Revolt: The Muskogees' Struggle for a New World. (Boston: Beacon Press), 1993.

Martin, Sidney Walter. Florida during the Territorial Days. (Philadelphia: Porcupine Press), 1974.

Merrell, James H. The Indians' New World. (New York & London: W.W. Norton & Company), 1991.

Nash, Gary B. Red, White, and Black: The Peoples of Early America. (New Jersey: Prentice-Hall, Inc), 1982.

Orrmont, Arthur. Diplomat in Warpaint: Chief Alexander McGillivray of the Creeks. (London: Abelard - Schuman), 1967.

O' Donnell, James H. Southern Indians in the American Revolution. (Knoxville: University of Tennessee Press), 1973.

Pearce, Roy Harvey. Savagism and Civilization: A Study of the Indian and the American Mind. (University of California Press: Berkeley), 1988.

Pickett, Albert James. History of Alabama, and Incidentally of Georgia and Mississippi. 2 vols. Charleston: Walker and James, 1851; reprint, Birmingham, Alabama: Birmingham Book and Magazine Company, 1962

Pine, L. G. The Highland Clans. (Tokyo and Vermont: Charles E. Tuttle, Inc.), 1972.

Pound, Merritt B. Benjamin Hawkins - Indian Agent. (Athens, Georgia: University of Georgia Press), 2009.

Prucha, Francis Paul. The Great Father: The United States Government and the American Indians. (Lincoln: University of Nebraska Press), 1984.

Reid, John Phillip. A Better Kind of Hatchet: Law, Trade, and Diplomacy in the Cherokee Nation during the Early Years of European Contact. (University Pack and London: Pennsylvania State University Press), 1976.

Richter, Daniel K. and Merrell, James H. Beyond the Covenant Chain: The Iroquois and Their Neighbors in Indian North America, 1600 – 1800. (Syracuse, New York: Syracuse University Press), 1987.

Rowland, Arthur Ray. A Bibliography of the Writings on Georgia History, 1900-1970. (Spartanburg, North Carolina: Reprint Company), 1978.

Schouler, James. History of the United States of America, Under the Constitution. (New York: Dodd, Mead & Company Publishers), 1880.

Shofner, Jerrel. Florida Portrait: A Pictorial History of Florida. (Sarasota, Florida: Pineapple Press, Inc), 1990.

Smout, T. C., A History of the Scottish People, 1560 – 1830. (London: Collins Clear Type Press), 1969.

Snow, Dean R. The Iroquois. (Oxford and Cambridge: Blackwell Publishers), 1994.

Strayer, Joseph R. On the Medieval Origins of the Modern State. (Princeton, New Jersey: Princeton University Press), 1973.

Strickland, Rennard, Fire and the Spirits. (Norman, Oklahoma: University of Oklahoma Press), 1975.

Sturtevant, William C. A Creek Source Book. (New York & London: Garland Publishing, Inc), 1987.

Sturtevant, William C. ed. and Washburn, Wilcomb E. ed. History of Indian-White Relations. vol. #4 (Washington: Smithsonian Institution), 1988.

Swanton, John R. Early History of the Creek Indians and their Neighbors. (Washington: Johnson Reprint Corporation), 1970.

_____. The Indians of the Southeastern United States. (Washington: United States Government Printing Office), 1946.

_____. Social Organization and Social Usage's of the Indians of the Creek Confederacy. (Washington: United States Government Printing Office), 1924.

_____. Source Material for the Social and Ceremonial Life of the Choctaw Indians. Bureau of American Ethnology Bulletin, no. 103 (Washington: United States Government Printing Office), 1931.

Sword, Wiley. President Washington's Indian War: The Struggle for the Old Northwest, 1790 – 1795. (Norman, Oklahoma: University of Oklahoma Press), 1993.

Szasz, Margaret Connell, Between Indian and White Worlds: The Cultural Broker. (Norman and London: University of Oklahoma Press), 2001.

Unrau, William E., Mixed-Bloods and Tribal Dissolution. (Topeka, Kansas: University Press of Kansas), 1989.

Usner, Daniel H. Jr., <u>Indians, Settlers, & Slaves in a Frontier Exchange Economy</u>. (Chapel Hill, North Carolina: University of North Carolina Press), 1990.

Waldman, Carl, <u>Atlas of the North American Indian</u>. (New York: Facts on File), 1985.

Wallace, Anthony F. C., <u>The Death and Rebirth of the Seneca</u>. (New York: Random House), 1972.

_____. <u>Religion: An Anthropological View</u>. (New York: Random House), 1966.

Watson, Thomas. "The Troubled Advance of Panton, Leslie and Company into Spanish West Florida." <u>Eighteenth Century Florida and the Revolutionary South</u>. Samuel Proctor ed. (Gainesville, Florida: The University Presses of Florida), 1978.

Weiten, Wayne. <u>Psychology: Themes and Variations</u>. 7th edition (New York: Wadsworth Publishing), 2007.

White, Richard, <u>The Middle Ground: Indians, Empires, and Republics in the Great Lakes Region, 1650-1815</u>. (Cambridge: Cambridge University Press), 1991.

Wood, Peter H. <u>Black Majority: Negroes in Colonial South Carolina from 1670 through the Stono Rebellion</u>. (New York: W. W. Norton & Company), 1996.

Woodward, Thomas. <u>Reminiscences of the Creek or Mushoghe Indians</u>. (Mobile, Alabama: Southern University Press), 1865.

Wright, J. Leitch Jr., <u>Creeks & Seminoles: The Destruction and Regeneration of the Muscogulge People</u>. (Lincoln and London: University of Nebraska Press), 1986.

Wright, J. Leitch Jr., <u>Florida in the American Revolution</u>. (Gainesville, Florida: The University of Presses of Florida), 1975.

_____. <u>The Only Land They Knew: The Tragic Story of the American Indians in the Old South</u>. (New York: Macmillan Publishing Company Inc), 1981.

_____. William Augustus Bowles: Director General of the Creek Nation. (Athens, Georgia: University of Georgia Press), 1967.

Vogel, Virgil J., American Indian Medicine. (University of Oklahoma Press: Norman and London), 1970.

Young, Mary Elizabeth. Redskins, Ruffleshirts and Rednecks: Indian allotments in Alabama and Mississippi, 1830-1860. (Norman, Oklahoma: University of Oklahoma Press), 1961.

Bibliography

♦

Secondary Sources: Journal Articles

Bennett, Gordon I. "Aboriginal Title in the Common Law: A Stony Path Through Feudal Doctrine." Buffalo Law Review 27 (Fall 1978): 617-636.

Booker, Karen M., Hudson, Charles M., and Rankin, Robert L. "Place Name Identification and Multilingualism in the Sixteenth-Century Southeast." Ethnohistory 39: 4 (Fall 1992): 339-402.

Chalker, Fussell M. "Highlands Scots in the Georgia Lowlands." Georgia Historical Quarterly LX (Spring 1976): 35-42.

Clinebell, John Howard & Thomson, Jim. "The Rights of Native Americans Under International Law." Buffalo Law Review (Fall 1978): 669-714.

Crane, Verner W. "The Origins of the Name of the Creek Indians." Mississippi Valley Historical Review 5 (December 1918): 339-342.

DeVorsey, Louis. "Indian Boundaries in Colonial Georgia." Georgia Historical Quarterly 54 (Spring 1970): 63-78.

Dowd, Gregory E. "Thinking and Believing: Nativism and Unity in the Ages of Pontiac and Tecumseh." American Indian Quarterly (Summer 1992): 309-331.

Downes, Randolph C. "Creek-American Relations, 1782 - 1790." Georgia Historical Quarterly 21 (June 1937): 142-184.

Downs, Dorothy. "British Influences on Creek and Seminole Men's Clothing, 1733 - 1858." Florida Anthropologist 33 (June 1980): 46-65.

Foreman, Carolina Thomas. "Alexander McGillivray." Chronicles of Oklahoma 8 (March 1929): 106-120.

Galloway, Patricia. "So Many Little Republics: British Negotiations with the Choctaw Confederacy, 1765." Ethnohistory 41: 4 (fall 1994): 513-531.

Hagedorn, Nancy L. "A friend to Go Between Them': The Interpreter as Cultural Broker During Anglo - Iroquois Council, 1740 – 70." Ethnohistory 35: 1 (Winter 1988): 60-79.

Holmes, Jack D. L. "Spanish Treaties with West Florida Indians, 1784 – 1802." Florida Historical Quarterly 68 (October 1969): 140-154.

Kawashima, Yasuhide. "Forest Diplomats: The Role of Interpreters in Indian-White Relations on the Early American Frontier." American Indian Quarterly 13 (Winter 1989): 1-14.

Kidwell, Clara Sue. "Indian Women as Cultural Mediators." Ethnohistory 39: 2 (Spring 1992): 97-105.

Kinnaird, Lawrence. "International Rivalry in the Creek Country: Part I, The Ascendency of Alexander McGillivray, 1783 - 1789." Florida Historical Quarterly 10 (October 1931): 59-85.

Kinnaird, Lucia Burk. "The Rock Landing Conference of 1789." North Carolina Historical Review. 9 (October 1932): 349-365.

Merrell, James H. "The Indians' New World: The Catawba Experience." William and Mary Quarterly XLI (October 1984): 537-565.

Morgan, Edmund S. "Slavery and Freedom: The American Paradox." Journal of American History 59 (June 1972): 5-29.

Miller, Christopher L. "Indian Patriotism: Warriors vs. Negotiators." American Indian Quarterly 17: 3 (Summer 1993): 343-349.

Nash, Gary B. "The Image of the Indian in the Southern Colonial Mind." William and Mary Quarterly 29 (April 1972): 197-230.

Neeley, Mary Ann Oglesby. "Lachlan McGillivray: A Scot on the Alabama Frontier." Alabama Historical Quarterly (Spring 1974): 5-14.

O' Donnell, James H. "Alexander McGillivray: Training for Leadership, 1777 - 1783." Georgia Historical Quarterly 49 (June 1965): 172-186.

O' Shea, John M. and Ludwickson, John. "Omaha Chieftainship in the Nineteenth Century." Ethnohistory 39: 3 (Summer 1992): 315-319.

Pickett, Albert James. "McGillivray of the Creeks." Alabama Historical Quarterly 1 (Summer 1930): 126-148.

Richter, Daniel K. "Cultural Brokers and Intercultural Politics: New York - Iroquois Relation, 1664-1701." Journal of American History 75 (June 1988): 40-67.

_____. "War and Culture: The Iroquois Experience." William and Mary Quarterly XL (October 1983): 528-559.

Thompson, Joseph J. "Law Amongst the Aborigines of the Mississippi Valley." Illinois Law Quarterly 6 (December 1923): 204-223.

Trigger, Bruce G. "Early Native American responses to European Contact: Romantic Versus Rationalistic Interpretations." Journal of American History 77 (March 1991): 1195-1215.

Wang, Xiao-Lun. "Cultural Mediators or Marginal Persons." Geographical Review 81: 3 (July 1991): 292.

Watson, Thomas D. "Strivings For Sovereignty: Alexander McGillivray, Creek Warfare, and Diplomacy." Florida Historical Quarterly 58 (April 1980): 400-414.

Whitaker, Arthur Preston. "Alexander McGillivray, 1783-1789." North Carolina Historical Review 5 (April 1928): 181-203.

_____. "Alexander McGillivray, 1783-1789." North Carolina Historical Review 5 (July 1928): 289-309.

Wright, Leith J. Jr. "Creek - American Treaty of 1790: Alexander
     McGillivray and the Diplomacy of the Old Southwest."
     Georgia Historical Quarterly 21 (December 1967): 379-
     400.

Bibliography

◆

Secondary Sources: Theses & Dissertations

Braund, Kathryn E. Holland. "Mutual Convenience -- Mutual Dependence: The Creeks, Augusta, and the Deerskin Trade, 1733 – 1783." Ph. D. dissertation, Florida State University, 1986.

Kennedy, Thomas John. "The Origins of Creek Indian Nationalism: Contact, Diplomacy, Clans, and Intermarriage During the Colonial and Early National Periods." M. A. Thesis, University of Houston, 1992.

Morse, Marian F. "Alexander McGillivray who put not his trust in Princes." M. A. Thesis, Florida State College for Women, 1936.

Neeley, Mary Ann Oglesby. "Alexander McGillivray, Diplomatic Leader of the Creeks: 1783-1793." M. A. Thesis, Auburn University, 1973.

It is said that the American is the perfect mean between the European and the Indian.

-   Moreau de St. Mery*

*James Axtell, The European and the Indian: Essays in the Ethnohistory of Colonial North America (New York, Oxford: Oxford University Press, 1981), 1.

Treaty of New York – 1790*

GEORGE WASHINGTON, PRESIDENT OF THE UNITED STATES OF AMERICA.

To all to whom those Presents shall come, Greeting: Whereas a treaty of peace and friendship between the United States of America & the Creek Nation of Indians was made and concluded on the seventh day of the present month of August, by HENRY KNOX, Secretary for the Department of War, who was duly authorized thereto by the President of the United States, with the advice and consent of the Senate on the one part, and the Kings, Chiefs, and Warriors of the said Creek Nation, whose names are thereu

A TREATY of PEACE and FRIENDSHIP, made and concluded between the President of the United States of America, on the part and behalf of the said States, and the undersigned Kings, Chiefs, and, Warriors of the Creek Nation of Indians, on the part and behalf of the said Nation.

The parties being desirous of establishing permanent peace and friendship between the United States and the said Creek Nation, and the citizens and members thereof, and to remove the causes of war by ascertaining their limits, and making other necessary, just, and friendly arrangements: The President of the United States, by Henry Knox, Secretary for the Department of War, which he hath constituted with full powers for these purposes, by and with the advice and consent of Senate of the United States.

Article 1. There shall be perpetual peace and friendship, between all the citizens of the United States of America, and all the individuals, towns, and tribes of the Upper, Middle, and Lower Creeks and Samanoles, composing the Creek Nation of Indians.

Article 2. The undersigned Kings, Chiefs, and Warriors for themselves, and all parts of the Creek Nation within the limits of the United States, do acknowledge themselves, and the said parts of the Creek Nation, to be under the protection of the United States of America, and of no other sovereign whosoever, and they also stipulate, that the said Creek Nation will not hold any treaty with an individual state, or with individuals of any state.

Article 3. The Creek Nation shall deliver, as soon as practicable, to the commanding officer of the troops of the United States, stationed at the Rock Landing on the Oconee River, all citizens of the United States, white inhabitants or negroes who are now prisoners in any part of the said Nation. And if any such prisoners or negroes should not be so delivered, on or before the first day of June ensuing, the Governor of Georgia may empower three persons to repair to the said nation, in order to see the whole Creek Nation, their heirs and descendants, for the consi cede, all the land to the northward and eastward of the boundary herein described.

Article 5. The United States solemnly guarantee to the Creek Nation all their lands within the limits of the United States to the westward and southward of the boundary described in the preceding article.

Article 6. If any citizen of the United States, or other person not being an Indian, shall attempt to settle on any part of the Creeks lands, such person shall forfeit the protection of the United States, and the Creeks may punish him or not as they please.

Article 7. No citizen , or inhabitant of the United States shall attempt to hunt of destroy the game on the Creek lands. Nor shall any such citizen or inhabitant go into the Creek country without a passport obtained from the Governor of some one of the United States, or the officer of the troops of the United States commanding at the nearest military post on the frontiers, or such other persons as the President of the United Sates may from time to time authorize to grant the same.

Article 8. If any Creek Indian of Indians, or person residing among them, or who shall take refuge in their nation, shall commit a robbery or murder, or other capital crime, on any of the citizens or inhabitants of the United States, the Creek Nation or Town, or Tribe, to which such offender or offenders may belong, shall be bound to deliver him or them up to be punished according to the laws of the United States.

Article 9. If any citizen or inhabitant of the United States, or of either of the territorial districts of the United States, shall go into any town, settlement or territory belonging to the Creek nation of Indians, and shall there commit any crime upon, or trespass against the person or property of any peaceable and friendly Indian or Indians, which if committed within the jurisdiction of any state, or within the jurisdiction of either of the said districts, against a citizen or white inhabitant thereof, would be punishable by the laws of such state or district, such offender or offenders shall be subject to the same punishment, and shall be proceeded against in the same manner, as if the offence had been committed within the jurisdiction of the state or district to which he or they may belong, against a citizen or white inhabitant thereof.

Article 10. In cases of violence on the persons or property of the individuals of either party, neither retaliation nor reprisal shall be committed by the other until satisfaction shall have been demanded of the party of which the aggressor is, and shall have been refused.

Article 11. The Creeks shall give notice to the citizens of the United States of any designs which they may know or suspect to be formed in any neighboring tribe, or by any person whatever, against the peace and interests of the United States.

Article 13. Any animosities for past grievances shall henceforth cease, and the contracting parties will carry the foregoing treaty into full execution, with all good faith and sincerity.

Article 14. This treaty shall take effect, and be obligatory on the contracting parties, as soon as the same shall have been ratified by the President of the United States, with the advice and consent of the Senate of the United States.

IN WITNESS of all and everything herein determined between the United States of America and the whole Creek Nations, the parties have hereunto set their hands and seals, in the city of New York; within the United States, this seventh day of August, one thousand seven hundred and ninety.

In behalf of the United States, H. KNOX, Secretary at War, and some Commissioner for treating with the Creek Nation of Indians. In behalf of themselves and the whole Creek Nation of Indians,

ALEX. M'GILLIVRAY.

Fuskatche Mico, X or Birdtail King.

Cusetahs. Neaathloch, X or Second Man.

Halletemalthe, X or Blue Giver

Little Tallisee. Opay Mico, X or the Singer

Fuskatche Mico, X or Birdtail King.

Cusetahs. Neaathloch, X or Second Man.

Halletemalthe, X or Blue Giver

Little Tallisee. Opay Mico, X or the Singer

Totkeshajou, X or Samoniac

Big Tallisee. Hopothe Mico, X or Tallisee

Opototache, X or Long Side

Natchez. Natsowachehee, X or the Great Natchee Warriors Brother.

Thakoteehee, X or the Mole.

Oquakabee, X

Tuckadatchy. Scholesse, X or Young Second Man.

Chinabie, X or the Great Natches Warrior

Ocheehajou, X or Aleck Cornel.

Tuskeaah, X or Big Lieutenant.

Cowetas. Homatch, X or Leader.

Chinabie, X or Matthews.

Juleetaulematha, X or Dry Pine.

Of the Broken Arrow Chaweckly Mico, X

Choosades Hopoy, X or the Measurer.

Coosades. Muthtee, X the Misser.

Stimasutchkee, X or Good Humour.

Alabama Chief Stilnaleeje, X or Disputer.

Oaksoys. Mumageehee, X David Francis.

Done in the presence of Richard Morris, Chief Justice of the State of New York. Richard Varick, Mayor of the City of New York.

Marinus Willett. Thomas Lee Shippen, of Pennsylvania. John Rutledge, jun. Joseph Allen Smith. Henry Izard. his Joseph (X) Corness, Interpreter.

NOW KNOW YE, that I having seen and considered the said Treaty, do by and with the advice and consent of the Senate of the United States, accept, ratify, and confirm the same and every article and clause thereof. IN TESTIMONY WHEREOF, I have caused the seal of the United States to be hereunto affixed, and signed the same with my hand.

GIVEN at the City of New York, the thirteenth day of August, in the year of our Lord, one thousand seven hundred and Ninety. And in the fifteenth year of the sovereignty and independence of the United States. **GEORGE WASHINGTON.**

By the President,

THOMAS JEFFERSON.

By command of the President of the United States of America,

H, KNOX, Secretary for the Department of War

*Indian Affairs : Laws and Treaties Vol II (Treaties), Compiled and Edited By Charles J. Kappler LL. M. Clerk to the Senate Committee on Indian Affairs, Washington, DC : Government Printing Office, 1904

"A nation that forgets its past can function no better than an individual with amnesia."

-   David McCullough

About the author:

The author currently teaches in the social sciences and is a freelance writer.

Other works of interest in Ethnohistory

Axtell, James, Natives and Newcomers: The Cultural Origins of
North America. (Oxford University Press) 2000.

Blackhawk, Ned, Violence over the Land: Indians and Empires in
the Early American West. (Harvard University Press)
2006.

Brooks, James F. Captives and Cousins: Slavery, Kinship and
Community in the Southwest Borderlands. (University of
North Carolina Press) 2002.

Jacoby, Karl, Shadows at Dawn: A Borderlands Massacre and the
Violence of History. (Penguin Press HC) 2008.

Jennings, Francis, The Ambiguous Iroquois Empire: The
Covenant Chain Confederation of Indian Tribes with
English Colonies. (W. W. Norton & Company) 1990.

www.ingramcontent.com/pod-product-compliance
Lightning Source LLC
Chambersburg PA
CBHW071152290526
45788CB00001BA/402